Praise for *The Complete Guide*

"If you have time to read only one book about reverse mortgages this is it."

—**Peggy Gardner, J.D., C.P.A.,** President,
Estate Planning Council of Colorado Springs

"I predict *The Complete Guide to Reverse Mortgages* will become the most widely used third-party resource tool for potential borrowers, their families, and the professionals who advise them."

—**Norman F. Peterson,** President,
Kirkpatrick Bank

"Every financial and retirement planning professional should read this book. This book unravels a complex and very important topic in a clear and entertaining style."

—**Raj Joshi,**
Financial Analyst and Advisor

"With the leading edge of nearly 80 million baby boomers set to hit the entry-age for reverse mortgages in the next year and reverse mortgage lending up 73 percent in 2006, this book is a must."

—**Robert Crandall, C.P.A.,** Member,
American Institute of Certified Public Accountants

"The one-of-a-kind graphics and clear writing style in the Kraemers' book unravel the mystery of how reverse mortgages transform home equity into useable retirement cash."

—**John N. Yates, CLU, CFP, ChFC and MSFS,**
Financial Planner

"*The Complete Guide to Reverse Mortgages* eliminates common misconceptions and distills a complex subject into an accessible resource for borrowers, their families, and the professionals who advise them."

—Robert Wrubel,
Senior Investment Consultant

"The Kraemers have taken a complex subject and made it very understandable."

—Diana Capoot,
Financial Consultant

The Complete Guide to

Reverse Mortgages

Turn Your Home Equity into Instant Income!

Tammy Kraemer and Tyler Kraemer

Avon, Massachusetts

Published by Adams Business
An imprint of Adams Media, an F+W Publications Company
57 Littlefield Street, Avon, MA 02322
www.adamsmedia.com

ISBN-10: 1-59869-215-1 • ISBN-13: 978-1-59869-215-0

Library of Congress Cataloging-in-Publication Data
Kraemer, Tammy.
The complete guide to reverse mortgages / Tammy Kraemer
and Tyler Kraemer.
p. cm.
ISBN-13: 978-1-59869-215-0 (pbk.)
ISBN-10: 1-59869-215-1 (pbk.)
1. Mortgage loans, Reverse. 2. Home equity conversion.
3. Retirement income. 4. Mortgage loans, Reverse—United States.
5. Home equity conversion—United States. 6. Retirement
income—United States. I. Kraemer, Tyler. II. Title.
HG2040.15.K73 2007
332.7'22—dc22   2007015753

Printed in Canada.
J I H G F E D C B A

This book is available at quantity discounts for bulk purchases.
For information, please call 1-800-289-0963.

Dedication and Acknowledgments

This book is dedicated to all of the passionate people who care about helping our aging population maintain a good quality of life and stay in the homes and neighborhoods that they cherish. We cheer you on during these changing times.

Thank you to Ed Clafin and Adams Media for believing that two heads are better than one even when those two heads are married. Reverse mortgages are often a family matter, and we felt that writing this book together enabled us to present a more complete picture of the emotional and financial challenges facing potential reverse mortgage borrowers.

We would each like to thank our coauthor for limitless energy and encouragement through another project together. May we continue to look outward together in the same direction, and keep our sense of humor.

Thank you to our two amazing sons, Kai and Cary, for teaching us why people get so attached to their homes; Lindsay Mulvey, for immeasurable assistance with the manuscript; Gregg Anderson, for the inspiring limerick; Gregory Daries, for making pictures that speak a thousand words; Jessica Hoover, for playing monkey and the barrel game while Mommy writes downstairs; Judy Fogler, for teaching that laughter improves all projects; and Sandy and Dorothy Kraemer, for providing never-ending inspiration and love to our family.

Contents

Introduction

> *There was a retiree named Joan*
> *Who had a reverse mortgage loan*
> *Some people might dread*
> *What might lie ahead*
> *But her path's a worry-free zone*

—Gregg Anderson, Financial Advisor and Poet

When most people think of reverse mortgages, they think of Joan as a 75-year-old widow living alone in a small 1930s bungalow near an outdated shopping center. You see her at the grocery store scanning carefully for coupon items. Many reverse mortgage borrowers fit this stereotype of Joan. Today, however, Joan might be a business owner who shops at an expensive organic grocery store or a couple with two well-educated children but no retirement nest egg. She could be many other people, maybe even you.

While each Joan is unique, the common thread is that she is one of 20 million or more Americans over the age of 62 who own their own home. The total home equity held by this group of people has been estimated at approximately $2.5 trillion. As home values grow and life spans increase, many of these house-rich people are looking for ways to use their home equity as a retirement asset.

x The Complete Guide to Reverse Mortgages

A reverse mortgage allows a homeowner to convert some of his or her home equity into a usable retirement asset while continuing to live in the home. Thousands of Americans have already learned about the advantages of reverse mortgages, and many thousands more will learn about them in coming years because of their growing popularity. To understand this trend, consider the statistics:

The Federal Housing Administration (FHA) insured only 157 of its popular home equity conversion reverse mortgages in 1990. In the first half of 2006, the FHA had already insured 55,000. As the number of older Americans grows, so does the number of Americans who would like to tap their home equity for living expenses, health-care costs, or to satisfy a lifelong dream. A reverse mortgage can also provide the peace of mind that many Americans are looking for in a time when uncertainty surrounds the traditional safety nets such as private pension plans and Social Security.

Federal Reserve Chairman Ben Bernanke recently called Social Security and Medicare "unsustainable." He then emphasized the major strains the nation's aging population will place on government programs. Government officials recognize the problem and are working toward a solution, but right now it is unclear how federal and state governments will manage the economic effects. What is clear, however, is that every American facing the challenges and opportunities of aging needs to take personal responsibility for his or her financial well-being.

For homeowners, that means understanding how their home fits into their retirement planning. It also means that professionals who advise these homeowners on financial and retirement planning (including CPAs, financial planners, real estate brokers, stockbrokers, life insurance agents, and attorneys) need to understand the pros and cons of reverse mortgages. Finally, it means that children of aging parents need to know enough about reverse mortgages to assist their parents in making informed decisions.

Reverse mortgage analysis can be complex, and the emotional and familial ties to our homes can compound the complexities. This book is meant to demystify the reverse mortgage and the process of getting one. Whether you are a potential borrower, a professional adviser, or a family member of a potential borrower, this book is written to empower you with the right information to make confident decisions.

The Complete Guide to Reverse Mortgages is broken down into five parts. Part I provides a history of reverse mortgages and explains some of the basics, including general eligibility requirements, costs, and payment options. Part II goes into more detail about the three most common types of reverse mortgages: the Home Equity Conversion Mortgage, the Fannie Mae Home Keeper, and the Financial Freedom Cash Account Advantage Plan. Part III focuses on personal planning. We cover important questions meant to help potential borrowers bring out the personal thoughts and financial information needed to decide whether a reverse mortgage is right for their circumstances. In Part IV, we look at what it takes to apply for and close a reverse mortgage. Finally, in Part V, we discuss post-closing obligations and special circumstances.

Throughout the book you will find graphics that demonstrate and reinforce concepts. As lawyers, we have found that one effective graphic image can be worth sixty minutes of explanation. Of course, we cannot imagine why someone would not want to spend an hour with their lawyer if they could! Nonetheless, our clients seem to really appreciate graphics and shorter meetings. We hope you do, too, and we hope you find the entire book to be a valuable resource in making your retirement years as worry free as possible.

Part I | The ABCs of Reverse Mortgages

CHAPTER 1

The Reverse Mortgage Story

Stories are meant to be entertaining, but they are also instructive. From humble beginnings to scandal and a happy ending, this story provides a framework for understanding today's reverse mortgages.

What Is a Reverse Mortgage?

Before we begin the story, you should understand a little bit about reverse mortgages or the story will not have any meaning.

> *A reverse mortgage is the true home equity loan.*
>
> —Ken Scholen, founder of the National Center for Home Equity Conversion and director of the AARP Foundation Reverse Mortgage Education Project

To understand the simple truth of Mr. Scholen's statement, think back to when you bought your home. If you purchased your home with the assistance of a loan, a lender evaluated your income and loaned you funds based on your ability to repay the loan. This loan is known as a standard or forward mortgage. In exchange for the loan, you granted the lender a security interest in your home to protect the lender in the event you did not repay the loan. Over time, you paid down and maybe even paid off the loan. As you paid down your loan balance, you built up equity in your home. Equity is the difference between the market value of your home and the amount you still owe on your loan. When you pay off your home loan, your equity equals 100 percent of the value of your home; you are said to own your home "free and clear" and you are entitled to the entire sales price minus closing costs when the home is sold.

A reverse mortgage allows homeowners age 62 and over to convert some of their home equity into cash without selling or moving out. Homeowners with a reverse mortgage remain living in their homes, retain ownership of their home, and receive tax-free cash disbursements. A reverse mortgage does not need to be repaid until the borrower dies, sells the home, or moves permanently out of the home. Over time, the reverse mortgage loan balance grows and your equity declines. That is why reverse mortgages are also known as home equity conversion loans; your built-up equity is converted into usable cash without having to sell your home.

Comparison of Forward and Reverse Mortgages

FORWARD MORTGAGE   REVERSE MORTGAGE

As the illustration shows, over time with forward mortgages, debt falls and equity rises as the loan is repaid each month. The opposite is true of reverse mortgages; over time debt rises and equity falls as loan advances are made and interest accumulates. For homes that continue to appreciate, the equity falls more slowly.

Now that we know what a reverse mortgage is, let's begin the story by introducing the characters.

The Beginning of the Story

> *The man with a new idea is a crank until the idea succeeds.*
>
> —Mark Twain

Nelson Haynes of Deering Savings and Loan may not have been thought of as a crank, but his idea certainly was new. Mr. Haynes is credited with making the first reverse mortgage loan, to the widow of his high school football coach in 1961. One can imagine the confused looks he received when explaining the idea to his lender peers. You want us to lend her money and we won't get paid back until she dies! Now he is viewed as a good person whose desire to help one widow cover her living expenses has helped many senior homeowners do so as well.

Another good person to know in the field of reverse mortgages is Ken Scholen. He has studied reverse mortgages and has advocated for government involvement and consumer protections since the 1970s. In 1981 he founded the National Center for Home Equity Conversion, a nonprofit dedicated to reverse mortgages. One of Mr. Scholen's most helpful contributions to consumers is his method of analyzing and comparing costs of reverse mortgages. This method is discussed later in the book.

Of course, a history lesson would not be complete without some bad characters. And, sure enough, early on in reverse mortgage history there were many instances of unscrupulous individuals taking advantage of seniors who did not clearly understand all of the terms of the loans. One early loan provision that received a lot of criticism was appreciation sharing. Appreciation sharing entitled the lender to a percentage of the increase in value of the home (known as appreciation) over the term of the loan. These provisions resulted in huge profits to lenders, especially for homes in communities with steadily rising home values, and dramatically reduced the amount of equity remaining for the borrower and the borrower's heirs when the home was sold. In some of the worst cases, the lender could take the title and force the borrower out of the home if the debt became greater than the value of the home. Other onerous provisions required borrowers to purchase annuities or other financial products in order to obtain the loan. All of these mechanisms reduced the amount of funds available to seniors in need and risked the security of their home.

A Better Reverse Mortgage

Things started to improve in the 1980s, when Congress created a government-backed insurance program for reverse mortgages. The Housing and Community Development Act of 1987 established a federal mortgage insurance program to be provided by the Federal Housing Administration (FHA), a division of the U.S. Department of Housing and Urban Development (HUD). HUD's job is to implement and enforce federal housing and community development laws. Under the 1987 Act, HUD was authorized through FHA to insure 2,500 home equity conversion mortgages (HECMs). That volume cap has been increased several times, and the current limit is 250,000 mortgages. A bill has been introduced to Congress that would remove the limitation on the number of reverse mortgages FHA can insure.

Today, HECMs represent more than 90 percent of all reverse mortgages. Because the federal government insures this product, it is considered the safest reverse mortgage. All FHA-approved lenders are eligible to participate in the HECM program.

Things further improved for reverse mortgages once the financial industry began regulating itself. The National Reverse Mortgage Lenders Association (NRMLA), founded in 1997, developed best business practices and a code of conduct for its members.

One best practice is to clearly distinguish between reverse mortgage products and the sale of insurance or annuities and to not coerce borrowers into buying additional products in conjunction with a reverse mortgage. Lenders are also directed to not recommend a product simply because that product generates higher fees; lenders are to make recommendations based on the product that makes the best financial sense for the customer.

Great Expectations

With advanced consumer protection and industry self-regulation, potential reverse mortgage borrowers now have access to vastly better information and products than they did twenty and even ten years ago. In fact, today you can hardly find an article on retirement planning that does not at least mention reverse mortgages. Financial planners now need to know about reverse mortgages in order to completely advise their clients about retirement planning options.

The government is as enthusiastic about reverse mortgages as are retirement planners. In its Strategic Plan for Fiscal Years 2006–2011, HUD identifies HECMs as a means to achieve its goal of helping low-income seniors secure living arrangements that are safe, affordable, and support independence. Because state governments are responsible for a large portion of Medicaid costs, they see reverse mortgages as a promising way to control costs by enabling seniors to cover more of their own costs, including covering the cost of preventive care that can delay or eliminate the need for assisted living.

In addition to low-income seniors using home equity for health care and other necessary expenses, wealthy baby-boomers are likely to use their home equity as a retirement asset. They may use the loan proceeds for long-awaited luxury items or trips or simply to maintain their preretirement standard of living. Because the funds can be used for any purpose, the possible uses for reverse mortgage funds are as diverse as the population itself.

Most analysts and commentators agree that although reverse mortgage activity is at an all-time high, the percentage of reverse mortgages is small compared to the size of the potential market. The proportion of the United States population that is 65 years of age and older is growing rapidly.

Share of U.S. Population 65 and Older

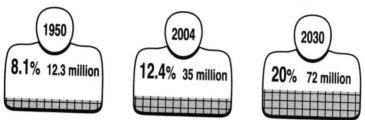

Data courtesy of U.S. Census Bureau; "65+ in the United States: 2005;" published December 2005

Almost 80 percent of these older Americans own their own homes, and many of those homes are owned free and clear of any mortgages. That amounts to nearly $2.5 trillion of home equity, based on a year 2000 estimate. According to projections from Wells Fargo, the reverse mortgage market could be as large as $74 billion by 2015. Many industry experts believe that the number of reverse mortgages will explode as consumers become more educated about the safeguards of today's reverse mortgages; specifically, that the most common reverse mortgages are non-recourse, which means the borrower will never owe more than the value of the house. The non-recourse nature of reverse mortgages is explained further in Chapter 2.

There are forces at work other than an aging population and improving consumer education that point toward a dramatic increase in reverse mortgages. Life expectancy is now about 80 years for men and 85 years for women. As life expectancies rise, so does the need for long-term health care. The future funding need for older Americans is enormous, and Medicare and

Medicaid cover only part of the cost. Most people would rather stay in their own home than move to a nursing home, but many find that the cost of staying at home is high, above and beyond out-of-pocket health-care costs. Even with a low mortgage payment, or none at all, fluctuating energy prices and unexpected repairs can stress most seniors' budgets.

While Americans are living longer and healthier lives, the reality is that the odds of having a disability or chronic illness increase with age. In a 2000 study, the U.S. Census Bureau found that 42 percent of people age 65 and older have a chronic condition causing disability, and 83 percent of those age 85 and older have multiple chronic conditions that result in functional limitations. According to a publication by the National Institute for Health Care Management, the number of people with multiple chronic illnesses is expected to increase by over 30 percent between 2000 and 2020. Chapter 6 explores in more detail the relationship between reverse mortgages and costs for long-term care.

To make matters even tighter, most researchers agree that somewhere between one-quarter to one-half of households are not adequately saving for retirement. Only about one-half of workers contribute to employer-sponsored pension plans, and IRA participation is even lower. According to a report by The Retirement Security Project, a nonprofit organization dedicated to improving the retirement income prospects of American workers, one-half of American workers near retirement have $15,000 or less saved. About one-quarter of workers who are offered 401(k) plans do not participate in the plans, and those who do participate rarely make the maximum contribution.

Low rates of saving, along with a rapidly aging population, longer life spans, and a rise in the need for long-term care, make the reverse mortgage an increasingly important retirement planning tool. Given the size of the potential market for reverse mortgages and the enthusiasm in the industry for making the products better, it is not surprising that the number of reverse mortgages is finally starting to move. Reverse mortgage volume was up 73 percent between 2005 and 2006. This is good news for consumers because the growth gives lenders more experience and competition for business.

More good news came in October 2006, when Ginnie Mae (a government-owned mortgage association within HUD that sells mortgages in the secondary market, which results in lower costs for borrowers) announced it had created a mortgage-backed security for home equity conversion mortgages. This allows issuers to securitize and sell HECMs and should increase competition among lenders. In turn, potential borrowers should see more product choices and lower costs.

Despite the fact that reverse mortgages make economic sense, especially in light of future need, there can be psychological drawbacks for certain would-be borrowers. The reaction people have to the idea of a reverse mortgage depends partly on their age and the generation in which they grew up. Many potential borrowers have spent a lifetime paying off their home mortgage, and asking them to reverse that process is counterintuitive. It can also wound the pride associated with building equity and passing on the value of a home, or the home itself, to one's children.

Considering a reverse mortgage can bring up all sorts of emotions and questions. The only way to overcome these feelings and make good objective decisions is through proactive education and communication. One thing is clear for today's seniors: planning for retirement depends increasingly on individual action. Since knowledge should precede action, let us now clear up some common misconceptions about reverse mortgages.

Misconceptions

Despite all the changes in the reverse mortgage industry, misconceptions still abound. These misconceptions explain the dismissive response a lot of people give when you mention reverse mortgages. Here is a list of five common misconceptions, each followed by the truth.

1. **The lender gets the house.**
   This is a widely held misconception. All the reverse mortgage products we discuss in this book are simply loans, which means that the borrower continues to own the home; the lender only has a lien against the home. A lien is a security interest against a property that secures the lender's right to repayment of the loan. The lender cannot foreclose as long as the borrower abides by the terms of the loan agreement, which typically means maintaining the home and paying the real estate taxes and insurance. Some of the confusion people have may arise from the fact that most borrowers sell their home if they move out so they can pay off the reverse mortgage loan.

2. **People only get reverse mortgages as a last resort.**
   In the early days of reverse mortgages this may have been the case, but today many borrowers are more likely to get a reverse mortgage because it fits with their retirement circumstances and goals. In fact, more and more people are taking out reverse mortgages to have a financial safety net for future expenses. Remember, though, that the high cost of a reverse mortgage means that careful planning should precede any decision to obtain a reverse mortgage.

3. **There will be no estate, and my heirs might even owe money.**
   First of all, a borrower's heirs should not owe money. The reverse mortgages we discuss in this book are non-recourse, which means the lender cannot collect more than the value of the house. Second, whether a borrower will have any estate to pass on to his or her heirs may be more complicated than just taking a look at the value of the home. In most cases, the allowable loan amount will be less than the value of the house. If the house continues to appreciate, and the house ultimately is sold, it is likely that the sales price will be more than the loan balance, resulting in some amount of cash that would pass to the borrower's heirs. Who gets what, of course, depends on your estate plan.

4. I can't qualify.

Unlike a conventional loan, the borrower's income and credit are not factors for qualifying for a reverse mortgage. The borrower's lender will run a credit report, but only to be sure the borrower does not owe the government any money (such as unpaid taxes). And although any existing mortgages or liens on the home must be paid off, the proceeds from the reverse mortgage can be used to pay off pre-existing debt. This reduces the amount of money available to you, but you still qualify for the loan.

5. The costs are too high.

Reverse mortgages are expensive, but cost is relative to the value you receive. If the borrower only keeps the reverse mortgage for a short time or uses the proceeds for an expense that could have been taken care of with another readily accessible resource, then the value may not justify the costs. On the other hand, if the borrower intends to keep the reverse mortgage for a longer period and use the proceeds for an expense that would be difficult to manage otherwise, the cost of a reverse mortgage may be well worth the value. Later in this book, we discuss value and ways to manage the high fees and costs associated with reverse mortgages.

Conclusion

Now you know the reverse mortgage story. There have been many improvements in the reverse mortgage industry, and you can expect to see many more. Starting with a clean slate, freed of misconceptions, it is time to get the facts about reverse mortgages. Read on to learn the basic anatomy of a reverse mortgage.

CHAPTER 2

Reverse Mortgage Basics

This chapter describes the basic terms and features that most reverse mortgage products have in common, including eligibility requirements, fees and costs, payment options, and consumer protections. Getting a basic understanding of reverse mortgage terms and features will make understanding the details in the product-specific chapters (Chapters 3 through 5) easier.

Eligibility Requirements

Reverse mortgages are far easier to qualify for than other types of loans. No one expects you to repay a reverse mortgage while you are living in your home, so you do not need steady income, perfect credit, or cash for a down payment. Remember, these loans were created to help older Americans convert their home equity into needed cash without requiring them to make monthly mortgage payments they could not afford. There are a few basic eligibility requirements:

- You must be age 62 or older
- You must own a qualifying property
- You must live in that property as a primary residence

Of course, there are some nuances to these basic criteria.

Age
The primary qualification for a reverse mortgage is that all borrowers are 62 years of age or older. If you own your home

with a younger spouse, that spouse also needs to be at least 62 in order to qualify for a reverse mortgage. A spouse younger than 62 years old can be removed from the title to the home, but this is not usually a good idea. Since the reverse mortgage must be paid off if the home is no longer the borrower's primary residence, the death of the older spouse borrower may trigger repayment and put the younger spouse in a difficult position. So, unless there is a dire financial need, it is probably best to keep both names on the title and wait until both spouses are 62 years of age to use a reverse mortgage.

Age also plays another role in reverse mortgages. Life expectancy is one of the factors lenders use to determine how much to loan to a potential borrower. The older you are, the more money lenders will loan you, because the term of the loan will probably be shorter. Many analysts agree that the best age for borrowers is somewhere between 72 and 75 years. At that age, you are old enough to receive a high loan amount and will probably live in your home long enough to justify the costs.

Homeownership

Another key eligibility requirement for a reverse mortgage is that you own your home. Renting and renting-to-own a home does not qualify. You do not need to own your home free and clear to apply for a reverse mortgage; however, the lender will require that all other mortgages and liens be paid off before or upon closing. In that sense, more equity results in higher loan amounts, since you will not have to reserve a portion of the proceeds to pay off existing debt. Now you have another good reason to make an extra loan payment each year to pay down your current mortgage.

There are a few basic financial requirements tied to homeownership, even though you do not need to own your home free and clear. These financial requirements are designed to protect the lender's security interest in the home. They are that:

- The homeowner cannot currently be in bankruptcy.
- There cannot be any liens against the property after closing.
- The homeowner cannot be delinquent on federal debt, such as student loans and federal taxes.

All of these things could jeopardize the lender's ability to get repaid from the proceeds of the sale of your home. The lender will want to be sure these matters are covered and that it has priority in receiving the proceeds from the sale of your home. You can pay off existing debt before you apply for a reverse mortgage, or you can use part of the reverse mortgage proceeds to pay it off. Before you jump and pay off current debt yourself, work through the numbers with a counselor to determine whether it makes more sense to use the reverse mortgage proceeds.

There are also some eligibility requirements tied to the type of home you own. The most clearly eligible property is the single-family home. Structures such as mobile homes, barns, and houseboats are at the other end of the spectrum and are clearly not eligible. Other properties that are typically eligible include townhouses, properties containing up to four units wherein the borrower occupies one of the units (a duplex, for example), and condominiums and manufactured homes that meet certain requirements. Chapter 13 covers the specific requirements that apply to condominiums, manufactured homes, and other uncommon real estate matters.

Primary Residence

The last of the main eligibility requirements is that the property must be the borrower's primary residence and not a timeshare or second home. Reverse mortgages help older Americans age in their home instead of a nursing home. To that end, you must live in your home for the majority of each year. Each loan has its own requirement for limiting the time you can live outside of your home, but most allow a few months each year for things such as travel or in-patient hospital stays. Obviously, selling your home or renting it will make the loan due and payable, since you are no longer using the home as a primary residence.

Basic Eligibility Requirements

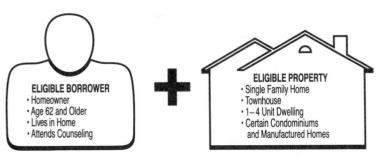

ELIGIBLE BORROWER
· Homeowner
· Age 62 and Older
· Lives in Home
· Attends Counseling

ELIGIBLE PROPERTY
· Single Family Home
· Townhouse
· 1–4 Unit Dwelling
· Certain Condominiums
  and Manufactured Homes

As you can see, the eligibility requirements are fairly simple. One potential advantage to using a reverse mortgage instead of some types of need-based assistance during tough financial times is that eligibility is straightforward and is not tied to using the funds for a specific purpose. The proceeds from a reverse mortgage can be used for any purpose. Most people use the funds for basic living expenses, health care, or home improvements, but they also may be used for travel or luxury items. Other options include single-purpose loans, which are discussed in Chapter 7 along with additional alternatives to a typical reverse mortgage. Single-purpose loans are a unique type of reverse mortgage in that the proceeds must be used for a defined purpose, such as payment of property taxes.

The Costs

As mentioned in Chapter 1, reverse mortgages do come with high fees and costs. The good news is that almost all of the fees and costs of a reverse mortgage can be paid from the loan proceeds. While this will save you the out-of-pocket expense, it will reduce the net loan amount available to you. Actual fees and costs vary depending on the lender and location of the property, but typical non-interest costs include these:

Fees and Costs

- Origination Fee
- Monthly Servicing Fee
- Mortgage Insurance Premium (HECM Only)
- Closing Costs
- Interest

After reading the list of fees and costs, you probably remember many of them from your forward mortgage. In fact, many reverse mortgage costs are the same as those incurred with any other loan. One difference is in the psychological impact of these costs. When you spend $150,000 to buy an appreciating asset, the loan costs seem minor compared to the large purchase price and the growth potential of the home's value. When you spend equity built up over a lifetime to obtain needed cash, every penny counts and detracts from the net loan amount available to you.

Another difference is that the costs of a reverse mortgage are actually higher than the costs of a forward mortgage. The high costs are due in part to the unique nature of the loan and the attendant risks. For example, the maturity date, loan balance, and property value at the time of repayment are basically unknown until the borrower leaves the home. In addition, there are a relatively small number of reverse mortgages being underwritten compared to the large number of forward mortgages that exist today. The high costs should come down as the reverse mortgage industry matures and lenders have more competition and experience on which to base lending decisions. In fact, as this book goes to print, Financial Freedom, a reverse mortgage lender we discuss in Chapter 5, is introducing a modified HECM known as the HECM Advantage that offers lower costs and therefore more net cash to the borrower.

Fees and costs can vary depending on the type of reverse mortgage product, the lender, and the county in which the property is located. Midway through 2006, the average value of a home in the HECM program was about $255,000. Assuming a 74-year-old borrower with a home located in an urban neighborhood, this borrower might pay about $12,000 in up-front costs, and, over the course of the loan, she could pay another $5,000 in monthly service fees and $8,000 in periodic mortgage insurance premiums, for a total of $25,000 in fees and costs. These fees do not include the interest paid over the course of the loan. The paragraphs that follow dissect this total into specific costs.

Origination Fee

The origination fee covers the lender's cost of preparing your paperwork and processing the loan. Because the origination fee is tied to the lender's loan preparation costs, it may vary quite a bit among lenders. It may also be negotiable, so do not hesitate to shop around. At this relatively early stage in the reverse mortgage market, however, shopping around may save only a few hundred dollars and will not have a large impact if you finance the costs.

HUD regulations limit the origination fee for HECMs to the greater of $2,000 and 2 percent of the home value or 2 percent of the county's 203b limit (whichever is less). The 203b limit is a geographically based lending limit. It is the maximum amount that HUD will lend a borrower with a home located in a certain area. For a home with a value of $255,000 located in an urban neighborhood, the origination fee may be around $5,000 or more.

Note carefully that the HECM origination fee is a percentage of home value, not the total loan amount. This sometimes confuses borrowers because origination fees for HUD's typical forward mortgages are calculated based on total loan amount and are capped at 1 percent. When expressed as a percentage of the maximum loan amount, HECM fees tend to range between 2.5 percent and 5 percent.

Monthly Servicing Fee

While the origination fee covers the lender's cost of preparing the loan, the monthly servicing fee covers the lender's cost of maintaining the loan after closing. For example, during the course of the loan the lender may make loan advances, change payment options, send account statements, and pay property taxes and insurance premiums. FHA limits the fee to $30 per month for loans with annually adjustable interest rates and $35 per month for those with monthly adjustable rates. Like the origination fee, which also is tied to the lender's activities, these fees will vary within the FHA limits among lenders and may be negotiable.

If you want to finance the servicing fees, the lender is required to set aside a total servicing fee for the life of the loan based on the assumption that you will live to be 100 years old. This set-aside amount will be deducted from your total available loan funds at closing, but it will not be added to your loan balance until the cost is actually incurred each month. So, you do not pay interest on the set-aside until it is used. A 74-year-old single female who lives to her life expectancy of 86 years would owe a total of about $5,000 in monthly servicing fees.

Mortgage Insurance Premium (MIP)

In addition to fees related to loan origination and administration, borrowers may be charged a mortgage insurance premium (MIP) if they choose a HECM reverse mortgage. This insurance reduces the risk of loss to the lender in the event that the outstanding balance of the loan exceeds the value of the property at the time the mortgage becomes due and payable. It also guarantees that you will continue to receive loan advances no matter what happens to the lender who originated your loan, and that even if your loan balance catches up to your home value, you will continue to receive advances and will never owe more than the value of your home.

Proprietary reverse mortgage products like the Fannie Mae Home Keeper do not charge the borrower for an insurance premium. Instead, the lender manages the lending risk in-house by adjusting loan-to-value ratios and tightening lending guidelines. Despite the MIP, the HECM is the most-used reverse mortgage, so the premium must be worth it.

Closing Costs

Closing refers to the final steps necessary to complete the loan transaction, including signing all of the legal documents and securing the mortgage. The closing often takes place in person at a bank or title company. To close a loan requires the services of many people other than the lender. For example, different people conduct the appraisal and inspection, secure the title search and insurance, obtain credit reports, and record the mortgage. The fees charged by these service providers are known as third-party closing or settlement costs.

Since these costs are passed through from third parties, they do not vary that much among lenders. They do vary, however, by locality and property. A rough estimate of closing costs for an average property is $2,000. Many of the service providers require payment at the time they perform the services, but you can usually ask for reimbursement at closing and add the costs to your loan balance. Keep in mind that this reduces the amount of cash available to you. Also, because these costs become part of the loan balance, interest will be charged on them.

Disbursement Options

While the costs of reverse mortgages can be discouraging, the variety and flexibility of disbursement or payment options is encouraging. You can select a payment plan for the loan proceeds from the following options:

Reverse Mortgage Payment Plans

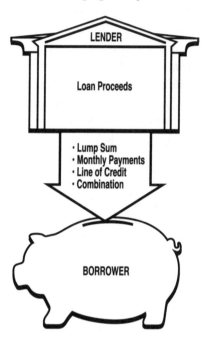

These different plans allow you to tailor the receipt of funds to your financial circumstances. A lump sum allows you to receive the entire principal loan amount at closing. Monthly payments can be structured as equal monthly payments for life (known as tenure) or equal monthly payments for a fixed period of months (known as term). With a line of credit, the borrower receives payments in installments, at times and in amounts of the borrower's choosing until the credit limit is reached. A combination might include a line of credit with either a tenure or term monthly payment.

Under most reverse mortgage programs, the borrower may change the type of payment plan throughout the life of the loan. More details about how payment options work with specific types of reverse mortgages are in Chapters 3 to 5. Analysis of how to select the right payment option for you is provided in Chapter 10.

Repayment and Termination

The appeal of reverse mortgages is that you do not have to make monthly payments to repay the loan. Reverse mortgages do not have a predetermined maturity date, as do conventional mortgages (for example, a 30-year fixed-rate mortgage that must be repaid 30 years after closing). Still, it is a loan that must be repaid at some point; it is just that the maturity date really depends on you. Most reverse mortgages do not need to be repaid until:

- The last surviving borrower dies
- The last surviving borrower sells the home or stops using it as a primary residence
- The borrower defaults or triggers the acceleration clause under the loan agreement

When the loan does become due and payable, the entire loan balance must be paid off in full. Most borrowers or their heirs sell the home to repay the loan. It is possible, however, to repay the loan with other funds. For example, a child may sell his or her own home to pay off the parents' reverse mortgage in order to keep the family home.

You need to carefully review the loan agreement for all of the conditions that make your loan due and payable, but fairly standard conditions of default or causes for acceleration include:

- Failing to pay property taxes
- Failing to insure or maintain the home
- Declaring bankruptcy
- Taking out new debt against your home
- Donating your home to charity
- Adding a new owner to your home's title
- Having the home impinged on by government action such as eminent domain, condemnation, or zoning reclassification
- Committing fraud or making a misrepresentation

If there is a default or cause for acceleration, the loan will become due and payable in full. The lender may require that the home be sold if you cannot pay off the entire outstanding balance. Most lenders will not jump to acceleration for a default. They would rather work with you to keep the loan going.

Of course, you may voluntarily repay the entire loan balance or part of it. Most reverse mortgages do not have prepayment penalties. Some reverse mortgage products, however, do not allow you to make partial repayments for the first several years of the loan. Paying off the loan in full may terminate the loan, so consider whether you want to keep a small balance to maintain the loan.

Consumer Protections

As discussed in Chapter 1, reverse mortgages are shedding their bad image. Some consumer protections are mandated by law, and others came about through industry self-regulation. You should only consider reverse mortgage products in which some form of the protections discussed in this section are in place.

Counseling Requirement

Every potential borrower is required to meet with a reverse mortgage counselor before the loan application can be processed. In fact, you will not qualify for certain reverse mortgages without presenting a signed counseling certificate. The sessions are usually free and extremely helpful for analyzing the different products and payment options. Counselors are independent from lenders and provide unbiased feedback to your questions. There is no excuse for not seeing a counselor.

Non-Recourse

There is no personal liability with reverse mortgages. Reverse mortgages are non-recourse loans, which means that the borrower or the borrower's estate will never owe more than the value of the property and the lender cannot require any other assets to be used to repay the debt. When the proceeds from the sale of the property are insufficient to pay off the loan balance, the lender must take a loss or submit a claim for insurance benefits to recover the deficiency.

Disclosure Requirements

In order to simplify cost comparisons among different types of reverse mortgage products and alert consumers to the real costs of reverse mortgages, federal Truth in Lending regulations (Regulation Z) require lenders to provide borrowers with a good faith estimate of the available loan amount and the total annual loan cost (TALC), which combines all costs into a single annual rate. This projection is to be provided in a table format with an explanatory statement. Typical loan costs included in the TALC calculation are principal, interest, closing costs, mortgage insurance premiums, and servicing fees. In addition to the TALC, the statement must include an itemized list of the loan terms, charges, age of the youngest borrower, and the appraised property value.

Payment Guaranty

What happens if the lender stops making the monthly payments that you rely on for expenses each month? Remember the mortgage insurance premium? It will protect you from default by a lender. With an FHA-backed HECM or Fannie Mae–backed Home Keeper, you are guaranteed to receive payments for the life of the loan, no matter what happens to the lender. Be sure that any reverse mortgage product you use contains a payment guaranty.

Interest Rate Limits

Nearly all reverse mortgage lenders charge interest on the loans based on an adjustable interest rate. This means that the rate may increase or decrease over time. These types of loans are known as adjustable-rate mortgages (ARMs). Though the rate will change, certain loans, such as the HECM, have caps or limits on the amount of change per year or over the life of the loan. Be sure to ask whether the product you are inquiring about has an interest rate cap.

Right to Cancel

Under Truth in Lending regulations, borrowers are entitled to a right of rescission, or the right to cancel the loan. Rescission is the undoing of a contract from the beginning (as if it never happened) and is different from termination, which can trigger repayment or other contract obligations. Lenders are required to provide a detailed notice of the right to rescind including a form for that purpose, so you can follow the instructions and use the form provided in the lender's notice.

Borrowers may cancel the loan for any reason up to three business days after the loan is closed or the lender delivers notice of the right to rescind, whichever is later. Business days include all calendar days except Sundays or legal public holidays. You must rescind in writing (not in person or over the telephone), and the written notice of rescission must be mailed, faxed, or hand-delivered to the lender's place of business by midnight of the third business day. The loan will not be funded until this rescission period expires.

Reverse Mortgage Products

We have provided a Reverse Mortgage Flowchart to help you review the basic principles discussed in this chapter.

Reverse Mortgage Flowchart

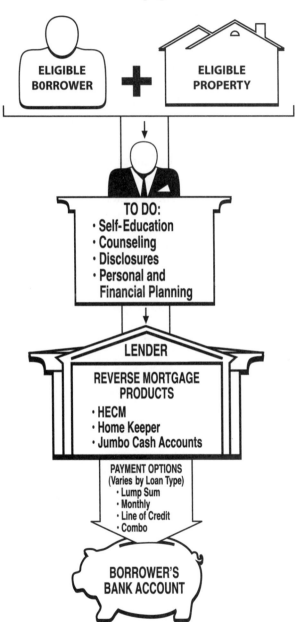

Now that you are familiar with the basics of reverse mortgages, we can dive into the details of the three most popular reverse mortgage products.

1. Home Equity Conversion Mortgage, or HECM—Chapter 3
2. Fannie Mae Home Keeper—Chapter 4
3. Financial Freedom Cash Account Advantage Plan—Chapter 5

Reverse mortgage products do sometimes change, so you should contact a counselor or lender to be sure you have the most up-to-date features and terms. After reading Chapters 3 through 5, you should understand each of these products and their differences.

Part II | Considering the Options

Home Equity Conversion Mortgages

This chapter describes the features and terms of the most popular reverse mortgage product, the Home Equity Conversion Mortgage, or HECM. Of all the reverse mortgages that exist today, more than 90 percent of them are HECMs. That is in large part because these loans are the only reverse mortgages insured by the federal government. Federal backing means that these loans are broadly available and have many consumer safeguards. HECMs are a practical option for today's older Americans wanting to draw on the equity in their homes.

Background

HECMs were created by the U.S. Department of Housing and Urban Development (HUD) to enable older homeowners to convert the equity in their homes into monthly streams of income or lines of credit. Under a 1987 Act, HUD was authorized through the Federal Housing Administration (FHA) to insure HECMs.

There are several reasons for the popularity of HECMs. First, HECMs are the most widely available reverse mortgage. They are available in every state, the District of Columbia, and Puerto Rico. All Fannie Mae–approved lenders must offer the HECM in addition to the Fannie Mae Home Keeper reverse mortgage (discussed in the next chapter).

Second, government backing means that borrowers are guaranteed to receive all payments due to them as long as the loan remains active. If the lender defaults or fails to make payments, then FHA will continue making payments directly to the borrower. It also means the lender is guaranteed to receive full repayment of the loan balance even if it is greater than the value of the borrower's home. This in turn means that the borrower's estate will never owe more than the lesser of the loan balance and the value of the home.

Third, compared to proprietary (non-government-backed) reverse mortgages, HECMs generally provide larger loan limits and charge lower fees. HECMs may seem expensive, but they are often less costly than other reverse mortgages. Because this may not always be the case, especially for people owning high-value homes or living in rural areas, you need to carefully compare the other options.

The sections that follow explain the features and terms of HECMs, particularly:
- Eligibility requirements
- Loan amounts
- Interest rates
- Disbursement options
- The costs
- Repayment and termination

Eligibility Requirements

The basic HECM eligibility requirements for borrowers and properties are similar to those for other reverse mortgages, but there are a couple of additional requirements. Because HECMs are federally insured loans, FHA standards apply as with any other FHA loan. In the case of HECMs, potential borrowers must:

- Be 62 years or older
- Own a qualifying property
- Live in that property as a primary residence
- Not be delinquent on any federal debt
- Meet with a HUD-approved counselor

Age

Each person listed on the property's title must be 62 years of age or older. As mentioned in Chapter 2, if a younger spouse is on the title, the borrower won't qualify for a reverse mortgage until the younger person reaches age 62. Removing a younger spouse from the title to qualify is not usually a good idea, since the death of the older spouse may trigger repayment and leave the younger spouse without a home. Before taking a drastic step like changing title to the property, check all of your options and alternatives to a reverse mortgage.

Property Type

To qualify for a HECM, your home must be a single-family residence or a one- to four-unit owner-occupied dwelling. Condominiums that are located in an FHA-approved condominium project are also eligible for HECMs. A condominium without prior FHA approval may be eligible by "spot approval" from an FHA lender, but only 10 percent of the units in a development can be approved. Planned unit developments and manufactured homes that meet FHA standards may also be eligible. Most cooperatives are not eligible for HECMs; no mobile homes are eligible. For a more detailed explanation of manufactured and mobile homes, please see Chapter 13.

In addition, your home must be at least one year old and meet FHA's minimum property condition standards.

The only collateral securing the repayment of your reverse mortgage loan is your home, so HUD must protect its investment by ensuring that your home meets its standards. Once you have applied for a HECM, your lender will send an appraiser to inspect the physical condition of your home. The appraiser will report both interior and exterior deterioration and damage.

If the physical condition of the home does not meet FHA standards, you may be required to fix the problems before closing. However, in most cases, you are allowed to use the HECM proceeds to pay for any required repairs after closing. If estimated repairs are greater than 15 percent of the maximum loan amount, they must be completed and approved prior to closing. Estimated repairs of less than 15 percent can be completed after closing.

If estimated repairs are greater than 30 percent of the maximum loan amount, your home may not qualify for a HECM. Sometimes your lender may require you to set aside HECM funds in an escrow account to ensure you complete the necessary repairs. The escrow amount is usually 1½ times the estimated repair cost, to be sure there is enough money set aside to cover the costs.

Primary Residence

The home being used as security for the reverse mortgage must be the borrower's primary residence. To occupy the home as a primary residence, the borrower must live in the home for at least six months of each year. At least one of the homeowners must reside in the home at the time of closing. During the course of the loan, the borrower may reside elsewhere for a maximum of twelve consecutive months due to illness. However, if at the end of that period the lender determines that the borrower is not likely to return home, the loan could become due and payable because the house is not owner-occupied.

Federal Debt

To qualify for a HECM, which is a government loan, you cannot be delinquent on any other federal debt (such as a Small Business Administration loan, federal student loan, or a VA-guaranteed mortgage). In addition, any existing mortgage, debts, or judgments that are secured by your home must be paid off at or before closing. Most people choose to pay off pre-existing debt (such as an existing mortgage balance) with HECM proceeds at closing. Finally, if you have been suspended or excluded from any HUD programs, you will not be eligible for a HECM.

Counseling

Each borrower must receive reverse mortgage counseling from a HUD-approved counselor or counseling agency. The counseling must take place prior to processing the loan application. The lender must provide a list of approved counselors in the borrower's state but is prohibited from recommending a particular counselor. The counseling session will cover the financial implications of and alternatives to a HECM. After completing the counseling, each borrower will sign and receive a counseling certificate that is valid for 180 calendar days.

In most cases face-to-face counseling is required, but telephone counseling is acceptable in certain cases where face-to-face counseling is impracticable. For example, telephone counseling may be used if there is not a HUD-approved counseling agency within fifty miles of the borrower's home, or if the local counseling agency does not provide counseling in the borrower's language. If a borrower is not legally competent, a court-appointed guardian or conservator or a person who has durable power of attorney may attend the session instead.

Loan Amounts

To minimize the risk of loss from non-recourse HECMs, HUD controls the total loan amount that borrowers may receive. The lender determines the total amount of money available to a borrower (known as the "principal limit" for the loan) by using a HUD formula that is based on three factors:

- The age of the youngest borrower
- The maximum claim amount
- The expected average mortgage interest rate

Age is critical to the lender because younger borrowers have a longer life expectancy, which results in a longer loan life. A longer loan life means that the lender will incur more costs to service the loan. Also, there is a greater risk that the loan's balance will exceed the home value when the loan becomes due.

The next factor, "maximum claim amount," is the lesser of the appraised value of the home or the current maximum loan amount that FHA will insure for a single-family residence in the geographic area of the home. The FHA maximum loan amount is governed by Section 203b of the National Housing Act and is sometimes referred to as the "203b limit." The limits are often less in rural areas than in urban areas, but they change periodically based on the cost of living and other factors. In January 2007, the 203b limits ranged from $200,160 to $362,790. Congress is evaluating whether to set one national limit for all HECMs, but until then, expect to be subject to these geography-based lending limits.

The final factor, "expected average interest rate," is not the actual rate charged to the borrower but is a rate HUD requires lenders to use to calculate the principal limit. For adjustable-rate loans, the expected average interest rate is the sum of the 10-year U.S. Treasury Security rate plus the lender's margin. The 10-year Treasury Security rate is used in a lot of financial modeling because it is the market's best current estimate of what interest rates are likely to average during the life of the loan.

HECMs have a feature known as a principal limit lock, which enables potential borrowers to lock the expected interest rate for a period of sixty days from the date of application. Since the expected rate is a main factor in determining the principal limit, the lock protects borrowers from receiving a lower total loan amount at closing if interest rates rise. Of course, you should choose a new rate at closing in the event interest rates decrease before closing, since you will be able to receive a larger loan amount.

The formula based on these factors yields the principal limit at the time the loan is originated. Unlike some other reverse mortgages, HECMs have a growing line of credit option, so the principal limit may increase over time. If the borrower selects a line-of-credit payment option, then the principal limit will increase each month after origination at a rate equal to one-twelfth of the sum of the interest rate in effect at the time plus the 0.5 percent mortgage insurance premium.

Interest Rates

Nearly all HECM loans are adjustable-rate mortgages (ARMs) because the companies that purchase these loans in the secondary market will only acquire ARMs right now. This means that the actual or applied interest rate may increase or decrease over the life of the loan. Since the HECM is administered by HUD, regulations define the formulas used to set the adjustable rates. HECM borrowers, however, choose how often the rate fluctuates. There are two types of adjustable rates to choose from: an annually adjusting rate and a monthly adjusting rate.

All HECM lenders must offer borrowers an annually adjusting rate. This rate is based on the current 1-year U.S. Treasury Security rate plus the lender's margin. An annually adjusting rate is subject to change once each year based on the increase or decrease in 1-year Treasury Security rates. For HECMs, the change is limited by regulation to 2 percentage points per year and 5 percentage points over the life of the loan.

Lenders may also offer a monthly adjusting rate. The monthly adjusting rate is also based on the current 1-year U.S. Treasury Security rate plus the lender's margin. A monthly adjusting rate is subject to change once each month based on the increase or decrease in 1-year Treasury Security rates. For HECMs, the change is capped at 10 percentage points over the life of the loan, but there is no limit on the amount the rate can change each month as long as it does not exceed the lifetime cap.

A change in the adjustable interest rate affects how fast or slow your loan balance grows. The loan balance is the total amount you owe the lender. The loan balance consists of the sum of each loan advance made to you plus interest and other charges that accrue on the amount borrowed. Lower interest rates make the loan balance grow more slowly; higher interest rates cause it to grow more quickly. Changes in the adjustable interest rate will not change the amount of monthly advances but, depending on the payment option the borrower selected, he or she may not receive any more advances once the loan balance equals the principal limit.

Disbursement Options

One of the best features of HECMs is the variety and flexibility of disbursement, or payment options. The options seem daunting at first, but learning how to use them is worth the effort. Tailoring the payment options to your financial needs is the key to success with a reverse mortgage. HECM borrowers may choose from five disbursement options:

- A monthly tenure plan
- A monthly term plan
- A line of credit
- A modified tenure plan
- A modified term plan

A tenure payment plan provides for equal monthly payments to the borrower for as long as the borrower lives and continues to occupy the home as a principal residence. Tenure payment plans work well for those needing extra monthly income on a regular basis. Borrowers may stop monthly payments for any period of time and resume them later. Having the flexibility to stop payments is especially important if you receive Supplemental Security Income (SSI) or Medicaid and need to meet the income and asset limits for these programs.

A term payment plan provides equal monthly payments to the borrower for a fixed period of months. The period of months, or term, is selected by the borrower. This type of plan works well for borrowers in need of extra monthly income for a while. For example, you plan to sell your home in five to seven years and move into an assisted living facility but need help with monthly living expenses while you are still at home. This option provides higher monthly disbursements than the tenure payment plan because shorter payment periods result in higher monthly disbursements. However, the payments will stop when the term ends, so plan ahead in order to cover expenses at that time.

The amount of a borrower's monthly disbursement under either a tenure or term plan is a function of the principal limit and the anticipated length of time the borrower will receive payments. Fewer and larger payments are tied to older borrowers and shorter fixed terms. More and smaller payments are tied to younger borrowers and longer fixed terms.

A line-of-credit payment plan provides for payments to be made to the borrower whenever the borrower requests a disbursement, until the line of credit is gone. Interest is not charged on undisbursed funds that remain in the line of credit. Interest is calculated only on the funds that are withdrawn. The borrower may request an advance in any amount up to the principal limit and may request the entire principal limit at closing.

One very attractive feature of the HECM line-of-credit payment plan is that undisbursed funds grow. The rate at which your line of credit grows each month is called the compounding rate. The compounding rate equals the current interest rate charged on the loan plus one-half percentage point divided by twelve months.

For example, if the monthly interest rate on the HECM is 5.5 percent, your line of credit would grow by 0.5 percent that month (5.5% + 0.5% = 6%/12 = 0.5%). If you had $100,000 in your line-of-credit account at the beginning of the month, you would have $100,500 by the end of the month ($100,000 × 0.05=$500). Leaving money in your line of credit is a great idea; you not only avoid interest costs but actually earn money. The line-of-credit payment option works well if you don't need all of the money immediately but want to have it available for emergency expenses, to cover a temporary loss of regular income, or to use for a special expense.

The modified tenure payment plan combines a lifetime monthly payment plan with a line of credit. Part of the principal limit is set aside for a line of credit that can be drawn on at any time, and the rest of the loan proceeds are received in regular monthly disbursements. Similarly, the modified term payment plan combines a fixed-term monthly payment plan with a line of credit. Both of these payment plans work well for those who need some extra monthly income and want a reserve available for emergency expenses.

Although borrowers must select a specific payment plan at closing, they may change the payment plan at any time and as many times as they choose. This flexibility is critical if your financial needs are likely to change a lot during the life of the loan. There is a nominal administrative fee (approximately $20) charged each time you change your payment plan.

The Costs

Like any other reverse mortgage product, there are non-interest fees and costs associated with originating and servicing the HECM loan. Weighing these costs against the principal limit available to you and alternative sources of income is central to deciding whether to use a reverse mortgage. The HECM includes the following non-interest fees and costs:

- Origination fee
- Closing costs
- A monthly servicing fee
- A mortgage insurance premium

The origination fee is a one-time charge that covers the lender's costs of preparing the initial loan application and processing the loan. The fees may vary by lender. The HECM origination fee is capped by regulation at the greater of $2,000 or 2 percent of the home's value or the 203b limit, whichever is less.

Standard loan closing costs also apply to HECMs. These costs vary depending on the type of property and the state and county in which the property is located. Typical closing costs include appraisal and inspection fees, document preparation and recording fees, courier fees, an escrow or settlement fee, inspection fees, attorney fees, and fees for a title exam and title insurance policy. Total closing costs usually run between $2,000 and $3,000.

Most of the closing costs can be financed and added to the loan balance. Some lenders may require borrowers to pay for appraisals and inspections out of their own funds, but you can request reimbursement and the costs will be added to the loan balance at closing. Note that adding closing costs to the loan balance will reduce the principal limit available to you, and you will be charged interest on these costs along with the rest of the loan balance.

There is still work to be done by the lender after the loan closes—for example, keeping records, printing statements, and processing payments. A monthly fee, which is capped by HUD, covers these servicing costs. The fee is currently capped at $30 per month for loans with annually adjusting interest rates, and $35 per month for loans with monthly adjustable interest rates. The exact fee, which may be less, is set by the lender at closing. The fee is added to the borrower's loan balance each month.

One cost that is unique to HECMs and may not be incurred with other reverse mortgages is the mortgage insurance premium

(MIP). This insurance premium ensures that you will receive promised loan disbursements and protects the lender from the risk that the loan balance will exceed the property value when the loan becomes due and payable. There is a one-time MIP premium that is due at closing, plus a monthly component. The one-time premium is equal to 2 percent of the home's value or 2 percent of the 203b limit, whichever is less. The monthly premium is based on an annual rate of 0.5 percent of the outstanding loan balance. HECM insurance is an FHA government program. In sum, the two types of MIPs for HECMs are:

- An initial, one-time, nonrefundable MIP of 2 percent of the maximum loan amount
- A monthly ongoing MIP based on an annual rate of 0.5 percent of the outstanding loan balance

The initial MIP for a $255,000 home would be $5,100, and the ongoing MIP could total about $8,000 over the life of the loan. The initial 2 percent MIP may be waived if the borrower uses the entire loan proceeds to purchase long-term care insurance. Whether it makes sense to use reverse mortgage funds to purchase long-term care insurance is analyzed in Chapter 6. While the MIP may seem high, it is what keeps this government lending product safe and sound for everyone.

Repayment and Termination

HECM borrowers may continue to live in their home during the term of the loan without repayment. When the loan does become due and payable, it must be repaid in one full payment, but that does not happen until:

- The last surviving borrower dies
- The property is no longer the borrower's primary residence
- The borrower does not occupy the property for more than twelve consecutive months
- The borrower breaches the loan agreement

When the HECM becomes due and payable, a loan servicer will send a repayment notice to the borrower, stating the terms of repayment. If the borrower is deceased, the servicer must provide adequate notice to the heirs or personal representative (referred to as an executor in some states) before initiating a foreclosure action. Usually, the borrower or the borrower's heirs have six months to sell the property before the servicer initiates a foreclosure action. Most people sell the property to repay the loan, but it can be repaid from other assets.

Since HECMs are designed to help older Americans in need, the lender will not terminate the loan for reasons other than death without HUD approval and without making an effort to fix the problem. For example, if a default is caused by nonpayment of taxes, the lender may use any remaining loan funds to make delinquent tax payments. The lender may also refer the borrower to a counselor who can help remedy the financial strain. If the lender or counselor cannot resolve the problem, the matter will be referred to the appropriate HUD field office. Disbursements to the borrower will continue until HUD approves the loan being declared due and payable. Foreclosure is not fun for anyone, so HUD and the lender will work hard with borrowers to avoid this step.

Of course, you may choose to repay the loan in whole or in part at any time; with HECMs there is no penalty for doing so. Repayment in full terminates the loan agreement, so before making this decision, be sure you will not need any more funds. If you are not sure, keeping a small loan balance might be a good idea. Otherwise, if you later decide you need funds, you will have to go through the costly process of applying for a new loan.

Partial repayments will keep the loan going, but you need to keep a couple things in mind. For mortgages with monthly payments in combination with a line of credit, the borrower must specify to which account a partial repayment is to be applied. If the borrower does not choose an account, the servicer will apply the repayment to the line-of-credit account. Applying a partial repayment to the line of credit will increase the line of credit available by the payment amount. Applying a partial repayment to the monthly payment account will allow the borrower to receive higher monthly payments. Be sure you figure out which option makes financial sense for you, and tell the lender in writing where to apply the payment.

Because HECMs are non-recourse loans, the amount of the full repayment will always be equal to the current loan balance or 95 percent of the current appraised value of the property, whichever is less. If the lender has to initiate foreclosure proceedings to sell the property, the costs of foreclosure will be added to and considered part of the outstanding loan balance. If the loan balance is greater than the home's value, the lender will have to accept the market value of the home as repayment in full. The lender may not pursue a deficiency judgment if the loan balance is greater than 95 percent of the current appraised value. The mortgage insurance premium will protect the lender in this case.

HUD's Home Equity Conversion Mortgage (HECM) is a safe and practical option for many older Americans searching for a way to make ends meet as their income declines and health-care costs rise. To locate a HECM lender in your area, contact your local HUD office or Area Agency on Aging. All HUD-approved lenders can offer HECMs; a list of HECM lenders can be found on HUD's Web site at *www.hud.gov/ll/code/llplcrit.html.*

Now that you have learned about the most popular reverse mortgage, read on to learn about some of the other options.

CHAPTER 4

Fannie Mae Home Keeper Mortgage

Proprietary reverse mortgage products are offered by banks, mortgage companies, and other lenders. Unlike HECMs, which have government backing, these products are created and insured by private companies. The reason you may want to consider one of these proprietary reverse mortgages over a HECM is that they may provide larger available loan amounts under certain circumstances (for example, if your home is worth more than HUD's 203b lending limit). Fannie Mae provides the most recognized proprietary reverse mortgage, the Fannie Mae Home Keeper Mortgage. This chapter describes the features and terms of the Home Keeper.

Background

So, who is Fannie Mae? Fannie Mae is a private non-bank financial services company that operates in accordance with a congressional charter but does not receive government funding or backing. So, it is considered a private company. The congressional charter directs the company to focus its financial services on low- to middle-income Americans.

Because Fannie Mae is not a bank, it does not lend money directly to borrowers. Instead, Fannie Mae works with lenders and insures the Home Keeper reverse mortgage similar to the way FHA insures the HECM. In order words, if your lender fails to make payments to you, Fannie Mae steps in to ensure you receive your reverse mortgage proceeds.

The Home Keeper is aptly named, since its purpose is to help older Americans stay in their homes as they age. The Home Keeper shares some traits with the HECM but has some unique features that may make it a more viable alternative for some homeowners. Fannie Mae started offering this reverse mortgage in 1995. It also offers a loan product called the Home Keeper for Home Purchase, which enables seniors to use equity from their current home to purchase a new house without having to pay on a new monthly mortgage.

Eligibility Requirements

Like the HECM, the Home Keeper mortgage has a few fairly simple eligibility requirements for potential borrowers and their property. There are slight variations in these requirements from those for the HECM, but they should not affect most borrowers. In order to apply for a Home Keeper reverse mortgage, you must satisfy the following requirements:

- Be 62 years or older
- Own a qualifying property
- Live in that property as a primary residence
- Own the home free and clear or have a small existing mortgage
- Attend a consumer education session approved by Fannie Mae

Age

As with the HECM, each borrower or person listed on the property's title must be 62 years of age or older. Unlike the HECM, the Home Keeper limits the number of borrowers to three people. If you are renting a room in your home, the renter will not count toward the borrower limit, because that person is not listed on the title. The most common scenario for more than two borrowers is one in which parents add their children to the property title.

If one child is on the property title with both parents, that child needs to be 62 years or older to qualify. The other hitch is that if the children are over age 62 and are going to be borrowers and remain on the title, they must use the home as a primary residence. If the children are not living at home and are on the title, they will likely need to be removed. Removing children from your property's title should be coordinated with your estate plan to make sure you are still accomplishing estate-planning goals.

Property Type

Fannie Mae's property requirements tend to favor single-family homes over other types of homes. On the other hand, because stringent FHA requirements do not apply to Home Keeper mortgages, as they do to HECMs, Fannie Mae may be more lenient in certain circumstances. The easiest way to resolve any worries you have about whether your home qualifies for this reverse mortgage is to talk to a local lender that offers the Home Keeper.

To qualify for a Home Keeper, the home must be a single-family house or one-unit dwelling, a condominium, or unit in a planned unit development (PUD) that meets Fannie Mae's requirements. Manufactured housing and townhouses may also qualify if they meet standard Fannie Mae guidelines. Two- to four-unit properties are not eligible, so if your home is one of these, you will need to apply for a HECM. Cooperatives are not eligible, either. Finally, properties requiring necessary repairs in excess of 15 percent of the property value may not be eligible.

Primary Residence

This requirement is almost identical to the HECM requirement that the borrower occupy the property as a principal residence. This means living in the property as a home and not vacating the property for more than twelve consecutive months. The residence requirement applies to all borrowers, including children who are on the property title. Again, the goal of these loans is to help people remain in their homes as they age.

No or Low Debt

As with other reverse mortgages, the home must be owned free and clear or there must be a relatively low remaining balance on an existing mortgage. Any existing mortgage debt must be paid off prior to closing, but the Home Keeper mortgage proceeds can be used to pay it off.

Consumer Education Session

Each borrower must agree to attend a consumer education session conducted by a nonprofit or public agency engaged in reverse mortgage counseling or by a Fannie Mae counselor. A member of the lender's staff may provide the counseling as long as it is separate from the loan application and origination process. The consumer education session must take place prior to the loan application.

The curriculum for the session must be approved by Fannie Mae. The session will cover things such as loan calculations and comparisons; costs and interest charges; eligibility and responsibilities; repayment and default; effects on taxes; estate and government benefits; and sources of disinterested consumer information on reverse mortgages. The borrower is welcome to have advisers or family members attend the session.

Total Loan Amount

Fannie Mae has a higher overall lending limit than does the HECM, which is constrained by 203b regulations. In 2007, Fannie Mae's national loan limit for single-family reverse mortgages was $417,000. This number usually changes each year and is based on the national average home price. The loan limit is 50 percent higher for Alaska, Hawaii, and the U.S. Virgin Islands. HECM loan limits vary by geographic location, but in 2007 the limits ranged from $200,160 in areas with average home prices to $362,790 in areas with high home prices.

Of course, you are not guaranteed to receive the maximum loan amount of $417,000. This just means that Fannie Mae will not purchase loans above this amount, so lenders will not make loans for more than this limit. A Home Keeper lender will evaluate three factors to determine the total amount of money available to you as the borrower (which is sometimes referred to as the principal limit for the loan):

- The age and number of borrowers
- The property value
- The adjusted property value

The age and property-value factors are fairly straightforward. Age is critical to the lender because younger borrowers have a longer life expectancy, resulting in a longer loan life. The longer the loan life, the greater the cost of servicing the loan and the greater the risk that the loan's balance will exceed the home value when the loan becomes due. That is why older borrowers tend to qualify for higher principal limits. Similarly, couples of the same age tend to have a longer combined average life expectancy than does a single borrower, so single borrowers tend to qualify for higher principal limits than do multiple borrowers.

Property value is based on the appraised value of your property, but Fannie Mae also requires consideration of an adjusted property value. The adjusted property value is the lesser of the appraised value of the property and Fannie Mae's loan limit. For example, if a home was appraised at $500,000 in 2007, when the loan limit was $417,000, the adjusted property value would be $417,000. Since your home is security for the loan, the lender will want to be sure its value is accurately factored into your principal limit. For that reason, the adjusted property value represents the amount of your property value that the lender can consider in calculating your principal limit.

Whether or not the borrower selects an equity share option will also affect the principal limit for a Home Keeper mortgage. The equity share feature allows borrowers to obtain greater loan proceeds in exchange for an additional fee at the time the loan is paid off. This additional fee or equity share is equal to 10 percent of the total property value. However, if the combined value of the loan balance and the equity share is greater than the appraised property value, the lender can only collect an amount equal to the appraised property value and will not receive the full equity share payment. This option may not be available in all states, and many lenders do not use this option due to the negative association most people have with equity share provisions.

In sum, a homeowner with a high-value home located in a county with a low HECM loan limit may be able to obtain more money from a Home Keeper because of Fannie Mae's higher loan limit. In areas where high-end homeowners are relocating from the center of the city to neighboring rural areas, a Home Keeper may provide more available funds than would a HECM.

However, high lending limits do not magically translate into higher principal limits. The lending limit is only one factor; it is possible that a HECM could lend more even with a lower limit. In fact, for average-price homes, HECMs tend to have the highest loan amounts. So, it pays to actually run the calculations for each loan to see which one results in a higher principal limit for a particular situation.

Regardless of which reverse mortgage provides a higher principal limit, there may be other reasons to choose one product over another. An obvious advantage of the HECM is its growing line of credit. The Home Keeper has a line-of-credit payment option, but unlike the HECM line of credit, it does not accrue interest. If the disparity in principal limits is not too great and you want to open a line of credit, it may make the most sense to go with an appreciating HECM. It pays to consider all of the factors, not just the principal limit, when comparing reverse mortgages.

Interest Rates

The Home Keeper, like the HECM, is an adjustable-rate mortgage (ARM) also known as a variable interest rate loan. The interest rate adjusts monthly and is based on the most current weekly average of secondary market interest rates on one-month negotiable certificates of deposit plus a margin determined by Fannie Mae. This means that the interest rate charged on your loan balance may change up or down each month. Interest rate adjustments affect the growth of the loan balance, but they will not change the principal limit or size of payments made to the borrower. In most cases, HECMs will have lower interest rates than do Home Keeper mortgages.

Home Keeper interest rates have a lifetime adjustment cap of 12 percent, meaning that the interest rate cannot increase by more than 12 percentage points above the original interest rate over the life of the loan. So, if the original interest rate is 7 percent, the rate could never exceed 19 percent. There is no limit to how much the interest rate may increase each month, as long as the change does not exceed the lifetime rate cap.

Disbursement Options

The Home Keeper reverse mortgage does not come with as many disbursement or payment plan options as the HECM, but it still offers a good variety of plans. For more detailed information on each type of HECM disbursement option, see Chapter 3. Home Keeper borrowers may choose from three disbursement options:
- A tenure or monthly payment plan
- A line-of-credit payment plan
- A modified tenure payment plan

A tenure payment plan provides for equal monthly payments to the borrower over the life of the loan. These payments continue until the loan is due and payable. The maximum amount available to a borrower for monthly disbursement is a factor of the principal limit and the length of time the borrower is expected to remain in the home, based on life expectancy.

There is not a term monthly payment option with the Home Keeper mortgage. Remember from the HECM discussion that with a term option you receive equal monthly payments for a fixed period of time. Borrowers can usually receive larger monthly payments with a term plan; however, the payments will stop at the end of the term, so you need a plan to cover costs once the payments end.

A line-of-credit plan provides for payments to be made to the borrower whenever the borrower requests a disbursement. The borrower may request an advance in any amount up to the principal limit and may request the entire principal limit at closing. The borrower may also draw funds, repay the borrowed money, and then borrow those same funds at a later time; this is known as a revolving line of credit. However, if the line of credit is repaid in full, it will automatically be terminated, so it is best to leave a small balance if you think you may need to use the line of credit again.

As mentioned earlier, the Home Keeper line of credit, unlike the HECM, does not have a growth feature. The amount available to you will remain constant over the life of the loan. With HECMs, any undrawn funds remaining in the line of credit will grow over time, increasing the amount of cash available to you. It will almost always be best to use a reverse mortgage product with a growing line of credit when selecting a line-of-credit payment option.

The modified tenure payment plan combines a monthly payment plan with a line of credit. Part of the principal limit is set aside for a line of credit that can be drawn on at any time; the rest of the loan proceeds are received in regular monthly disbursements. This payment plan works well for those needing some extra monthly income and wanting a reserve available for emergency expenses.

Borrowers must select a payment plan at closing but may change the payment plan at any time. Home Keeper lenders may charge a fee of no more than $50 for each payment change, although many of them will allow the fee to be financed and added to the loan balance.

The Costs

Like any other reverse mortgage product, or any forward mortgage for that matter, the borrower must pay a variety of fees and costs to take out and maintain the loan. Part of the decision to use a reverse mortgage is weighing these costs against the amount of money available to you through the loan. In addition to the interest cost that was discussed earlier, the Home Keeper mortgage includes the following costs:

- A one-time origination fee
- Closing costs
- A monthly servicing fee

The one-time origination fee covers the lender's costs in preparing the initial loan application and processing the loan. As it is for the HECM, the Home Keeper origination fee is capped. The maximum origination fee that can be charged by a lender is $2,000 or 2 percent of the adjusted property value or purchase price, whichever is greater.

Closing a Home Keeper loan involves as much work as closing any other loan, so there will be closing costs. These costs vary depending on the type of property and the state and county where the property is located. Typical closing costs include appraisal and inspection fees, document preparation and recording fees, courier fees, escrow or settlement fees, inspection fees, attorney fees, and title exam and title insurance policy.

Most of the closing costs can be financed and added to the loan balance. Some closing costs may have to be paid by the borrower at the time they are incurred, but you can request reimbursement and these costs will be added to the loan balance at closing. Remember that adding closing costs to the loan balance will reduce the principal limit available to you, and you will be charged interest on these costs along with the rest of the loan balance.

There are post-closing costs as well. The monthly servicing fee covers the loan servicer's cost of keeping records and processing loan payments. This fee also is capped by Fannie Mae. The actual fee is set by the lender at closing, but it will range from as little as $15 to no more than $35 per month. This flat fee is simply added to the borrower's loan balance each month.

As you may have noticed, the list of Home Keeper costs does not include a mortgage insurance premium. Fannie Mae manages this risk in-house, so there is not a separate fee charged to the borrower for insurance. For that reason, non-interest fees and costs are usually lower for Home Keeper mortgages than for the HECM.

Repayment and Termination

The same repayment principle applies to Home Keeper mortgages as to HECMs; borrowers continue to live in their home during the term of the loan and do not need to repay the loan each month. Home Keeper mortgages must be repaid in one full payment when they become due, but that does not happen until:

- The last surviving borrower dies
- The property is sold or title is conveyed to the property
- A borrower no longer lives in the property as a principal residence
- A borrower defaults under the loan agreement

The loan will be considered in default and the lender may require repayment in full if you fail to maintain the property or meet your obligations under the loan agreement (for example, paying property taxes and homeowners insurance when due). If the default is caused by nonpayment of taxes or failure to make repairs, the lender has the right to use any remaining loan funds to make necessary payments or repairs. As with HECMs, Home Keeper lenders will usually make quite an effort to work with borrowers who cannot afford to pay taxes or maintain the property before calling the loan in default.

There is not a penalty for repaying all or part of a Home Keeper loan balance before it becomes due. Some people may want to pay down the loan to rebuild equity in the property. Keep in mind, though, that repayment in full terminates the loan agreement, so before you make this decision, be sure you will not need any more funds. If you are not sure, keeping a small loan balance might be a good idea. Otherwise, if you later decide you need funds, you will have to apply for a new loan.

Since Home Keeper mortgages are non-recourse loans, just like HECMs, the amount of the full repayment will always be equal to the current loan balance or the market value of the property, whichever is less. If the loan balance is greater than the home's value when the loan becomes due, the lender will have to accept the market value of the home as repayment in full.

Home Keeper for Home Purchase

As far as Home Keeper reverse mortgages go, we saved the best for last. The most interesting Fannie Mae offering that distinguishes the Home Keeper reverse mortgage from the HECM is the Home Keeper for Home Purchase loan option. This offering combines a typical home purchase loan with a reverse mortgage. It allows persons 62 years of age or older to buy a new home that better suits their needs without monthly mortgage payments.

The eligibility requirements for the Home Keeper for Home Purchase are essentially the same as that of the standard Home Keeper. One additional requirement is that you have enough money on hand to make a sufficient down payment on the new home. If you do not have enough money saved or available from other sources, you may be able to use proceeds from the sale of your current home.

Like any other reverse mortgage, there are no income requirements and no monthly payments. For many retirees this may be one of the only ways to qualify to purchase a new and possibly more expensive home. Some practical reasons to use a Home Keeper for Home Purchase include purchasing a home that is more accessible, easier to maintain, and closer to family members.

The drawback to using equity to purchase a new home is that the funds are limited to the purchase only. You will not be able to use the reverse mortgage to receive monthly payments or establish a line of credit, so you must be able to cover your own living expenses through your life expectancy. The Home Purchase concept sounds simple and is certainly intriguing, but sorting out the math is rather complicated. If you are interested in this option, seek out a good counselor or financial adviser.

Summary of Differences

Fannie Mae's most unique offering in the field of reverse mortgages is the ability to purchase a new home with equity from your old home. Otherwise, the HECM and Home Keeper reverse mortgages are very similar. Still, as noted earlier, there are some differences. Following is a summary of the primary differences between these two reverse mortgage products:

- Home Keeper limits the number of borrowers per property to no more than three.
- Multifamily dwellings such as duplexes, triplexes, and four-unit properties are not eligible for Home Keepers.

- The Home Keeper has a single national lending limit, whereas HECM loan limits vary by location.
- Home Keepers do not include a mortgage insurance premium.
- Term payments (monthly payments for a fixed number of months) are not available for Home Keepers.
- The Home Keeper line of credit does not grow over time, as the HECM does.
- Different calculations are used to determine loan limits and cap interest rates.

To apply for a Home Keeper or Home Keeper for Home Purchase reverse mortgage, contact Fannie Mae at 1-800-7FANNIE or go to *www.fanniemae.com* to obtain a list of lenders in your area that are authorized to offer these loans. Lenders that offer the Home Keeper mortgage are also required to offer the HECM, so they should be able to help you compare the two loans. Fannie Mae's Web site also has informative fact sheets about both types of reverse mortgages.

CHAPTER 5

Financial Freedom Cash Account Advantage Plan

If you live in Manhattan, Santa Barbara, or Aspen, chances are pretty good that the value of your home exceeds the maximum 2006 HECM lending limit of $362,790. It probably also exceeds the 2006 Fannie Mae national limit of $417,000. Having a high-value home is typically a good "problem," but there are some challenges. There are not many buyers who can truly afford high-end homes, especially when interest rates go up, so selling the family home and downsizing in the same community may not be a simple retirement option. Downsizing in the same community is also financially risky if housing prices in the area have been overly inflated compared to the rest of the nation.

Jumbo cash accounts, with virtually no lending limits, can help residents retire in their higher-priced home by using their appreciated equity. These accounts can also offer peace of mind by insulating homeowners from worry about a fluctuating housing market. This chapter describes the features of one of the most popular jumbo reverse mortgages, the Financial Freedom Cash Account Advantage Plan.

Background

Financial Freedom is owned by Indymac Bank and is one of the largest originators and servicers of reverse mortgages in the United States. In 2005, it originated over $2.9 billion in loan funds and serviced about 77,000 loans. It offers the HECM and the Home Keeper as well as its proprietary Cash Account Advantage Plan. In order to help ensure that its borrowers receive honest, objective, and complete information, Financial Freedom has implemented "best practices" standards. Here are a few of the best practices:

- Requiring that all borrowers receive a disclosure document showing all of their reverse mortgage options
- Encouraging all of the borrower's personal and professional advisers to attend meetings with the loan originator
- Providing employees and affiliated originators with the most comprehensive reverse mortgage training in the industry, including training on how to protect the interests of their customers

There are other companies that offer proprietary reverse mortgages and jumbo cash accounts, and any member of the NRMLA should adhere to a code of conduct that compares to Financial Freedom's best practices. Because Financial Freedom is the largest reverse mortgage specialist, its Cash Account Advantage Plan provides a good example of proprietary jumbo reverse mortgages. Keep in mind throughout this chapter that the Cash Account Advantage is designed for homeowners with higher-value homes ($450,000 to $750,000 or more).

Eligibility

Like the HECM and the Home Keeper mortgage, the Cash Account Advantage has a few simple eligibility requirements for potential borrowers and their property. To be eligible for a Cash Account Advantage reverse mortgage, you must satisfy the following requirements:

- Be age 62 or older
- Own a qualifying property
- Live in that property as a primary residence

- Own the home free and clear or have a low existing mortgage
- Meet with a Financial Freedom-approved counselor

Most of these requirements are similar to those for other reverse mortgages, so they are not reviewed in detail again in this chapter. The main difference is that because the Cash Account Advantage is geared toward very high-end homes, Financial Freedom is more lenient in terms of the types of properties that are eligible. Qualifying properties include:

- Single-family detached homes
- Condominiums
- Planned Unit Developments (PUDs)
- One- to four-unit properties (assuming the borrower owns all units and lives in one)
- Manufactured homes with the underlying property
- Co-ops located in New York

As you can see from the list, Financial Freedom accepts a wider variety of property types than the HECM. It also does not limit the number of condominiums in a development that are eligible, as does the HECM (10 percent). So, if your condominium development is maxed on the number of HECMs that can exist in the development, a Cash Account Advantage Plan may be the only reverse mortgage option for you. Financial Freedom also accepts rental properties if the owner lives in one of the units, and manufactured homes if the borrower owns the property under the home.

Another difference that may impact your ability to use a Cash Account Advantage reverse mortgage is that these products are not currently available in all parts of the United States. They are available in most areas with the highest home values. In addition, as you will learn in the section on disbursement options, the only payment method for the Cash Account Advantage Plan is a line of credit.

Total Loan Amount

In many ways the financial mechanics of the Cash Account Advantage Plan are similar to the other reverse mortgages we have covered. The available loan amount or principal limit is determined by considering the value of the home and the age of each borrower. The big difference is that the Cash Account Advantage Plan has virtually no loan limit, which means that under the right circumstances borrowers will be able to convert a greater percentage of their home's equity into usable cash.

Financial Freedom continually innovates in an effort to provide access to more equity for seniors who have high-value homes. The Cash Account Advantage Plan was introduced in July 2006 with the highest principal lending limit in the industry. With the Cash Account Advantage Plan, a 65-year-old could access 75 percent more home equity than with previous Financial Freedom jumbo cash account offerings.

A great Internet-based tool for comparing the outcome with the different reverse mortgages can be found on Financial Freedom's Web site at *www.financialfreedom.com/calculator/input.asp*. Input your age, home value, Zip Code and outstanding debt, and the calculator will provide an estimate of what someone with those circumstances could borrow from each type of loan. Keep in mind that these are estimates of only the principal limits available from each type of loan. The calculator does not include a comparison of costs or other factors, such as the need for monthly disbursements.

The most dramatic difference in principal limits is at the high end. For example, the principal loan amount for a Cash Account Advantage Plan loan for a 71-year-old borrower who owns a home in Santa Barbara worth $850,000, without any existing mortgage debt, would be $346,507, compared to $211,388 for the HECM and $139,277 for the Home Keeper. The Cash Account Advantage offers this homeowner over $135,000 more than the other reverse mortgages.

The difference narrows at the midrange, because this product is not really designed for such properties. For example, if the same 71-year-old borrower owns a home in central Illinois worth $400,000 without any existing mortgage debt, she could receive $162,520 from the Cash Account Advantage Plan compared to $113,968 for the HECM and $134,049 for the Home Keeper. In this scenario, the difference between the Cash Account Advantage Plan and the Home Keeper is narrow enough that factors other than available cash may influence the homeowner's decision.

As you will see, though, if you input different ages, values, and property locations in the Financial Freedom reverse mortgage calculator, the results are not always what you would predict. Regardless of which reverse mortgage provides a higher principal limit, there may be other reasons to choose one product over another. Helping to weigh all of your needs against the product offerings to achieve the best value for you is a job for a qualified reverse mortgage counselor or financial adviser.

Interest Rates

Like other reverse mortgages, the Cash Account Advantage Plan mortgages come with variable interest rates that are tied to a financial index (these are referred to as adjustable-rate mortgages, or ARMs). In this case, the financial index is the 6-month LIBOR (London Interbank Offered Rate). The LIBOR is the rate at which banks in London lend money to each other, but it is relied upon in the U.S. financial markets as well. The borrower's interest rate is based on the 6-month LIBOR index plus a margin determined by Financial Freedom (3.5 percent) and is adjusted semiannually (every six months).

Financial Freedom interest rates have a lifetime cap of 6 percent, meaning that the interest rate cannot increase by more than 6 percentage points above the original interest rate over the life of the loan. So, if the original interest rate is 7 percent, the rate could never exceed 13 percent. There is no limit to how much the interest rate may increase semiannually, as long as the change does not exceed the lifetime rate cap.

Disbursement Options

A major difference between the Cash Account Advantage Plan and other reverse mortgages is in the choice of disbursement or payment options or, really, the lack of choices. The only payment option for the Cash Account Advantage Plan is a line of credit. With other reverse mortgages, the borrower can choose monthly payments, a line of credit, and even a combination of monthly payments with a line of credit.

While this may sound like a limitation, a line of credit itself can be very flexible. However, it does require more financial planning and fiscal discipline. A borrower could withdraw and then replace as much as desired, and as often as desired, subject to the requirement that each withdrawal be no less than $500. It is in the borrower's best interest, however, to only withdraw what she or he really needs, because the Cash Account Advantage Plan line of credit appreciates just as the HECM line of credit does.

The unused portion of the loan earns interest at a compounding rate of 5 percent per year. Compounding means that the 5 percent is calculated on all money in the line of credit, including earned but unused interest payments. That is more earning power than you could get on an average savings account or certificate of deposit.

While the Cash Account Advantage Plan is limited to line-of-credit disbursements, there are three options for receiving the funds via the line of credit:

- Credit line option
- Combo option
- Cash out option

Each option has its own disbursement requirements, fees and costs, and repayment restrictions.

Credit Line Option

This standard option provides an open-ended revolving line of credit. Revolving credit just means that once you repay an amount, it can be borrowed again. The origination fee for this option is 2 percent of the total loan limit or $2,500, whichever is greater. The minimum amount of each withdrawal is $500, and unused credit grows at 5 percent per year. There are no full or partial prepayment penalties. This option has the highest fees but provides the most flexibility.

Combo Option

This option requires borrowers to withdraw at least 75 percent of the available loan amount at the time of closing, and this initial withdrawal must be at least $200,000. After closing, each withdrawal must be at least $500, and unused credit grows at 5 percent per year. The tradeoff for taking so much cash at once is that the lender's origination fee is waived. The borrower is still responsible for all third-party closing costs. There is no full prepayment penalty, but partial prepayment of the initial withdrawal is not allowed for the first five years.

Cash Out Option

This option requires borrowers to withdraw 100 percent of the available loan amount at closing, an amount that must be at least $275,000. In exchange, the origination fee and the closing costs are waived. As with the combo option, there is no full prepayment penalty, but partial prepayment of the initial withdrawal is not allowed for the first five years.

While reducing loan costs through the combo option or cash out option sounds like a good deal, realize that you will be starting the loan with a large balance that will accrue interest quickly, and you will not be able to repay less than the full balance for five years. If you need a large sum of money right away, you may as well save some costs and use one of these options. Otherwise, take full advantage of the 5 percent earning power for unused funds and keep withdrawals as small as necessary by using the basic credit line option.

Equity Choice

Another really unique feature of the Cash Account Advantage Plan that is available with all three of these options is called the equity choice feature. Equity choice allows the borrower to limit the loan obligation to a stated percentage of the market value of the home, thereby protecting a percentage of the equity. In other words, it can relieve worries about how much equity will be left for the borrower or the borrower's heirs when the loan becomes due and payable. Borrowers can choose to protect a minimum of 10 percent up to a maximum of 50 percent of their home equity. Limiting your loan obligation, however, will limit the maximum available loan amount at closing.

The Costs

There are a variety of non-interest fees and costs to originate and maintain a Cash Account Advantage loan. The basic costs are similar to those for any other reverse mortgage. The difference is that some of the costs can be waived if the borrower selects the right payment option. These fees include:
- A one-time origination fee
- Closing costs
- A monthly servicing fee

The origination fee for the Cash Account Advantage Plan is capped, just as it is for the HECM and the Home Keeper. The cap is $2,500 or 2 percent of the maximum initial loan amount, whichever is greater. Note the difference in the computation.

With HECMs and Home Keepers, the origination fee is based on a percentage of the home's value with a cap or minimum; with the Cash Account Advantage Plan, it is based on the available loan amount with a cap. The origination fee is waived for borrowers who select the combo option or the cash out option and withdraw the required amount.

Closing costs for the Cash Account Advantage Plan are the same as for any other reverse mortgage or forward mortgage. These costs vary depending on the type of property, and the state and county where the property is located. Borrowers who select the cash out option and withdraw the required amount may not have to pay closing costs, except for applicable state and local taxes.

A monthly servicing fee is automatically financed on the Cash Account Advantage loan account each month. The fee is comparable to monthly servicing fees for other reverse mortgages. This fee does not apply in Illinois and Maryland.

There is not a mortgage insurance premium for the Cash Account Advantage Plan. Financial Freedom manages this risk in-house, so there is not a separate fee charged to the borrower.

Summary of Differences

The Cash Account Advantage reverse mortgage is very different from the HECM and the Home Keeper. It is aimed at helping borrowers with high-value homes, typically in expensive communities, unlock their equity. The unique characteristics of the Cash Account Advantage Plan are that:

- There are virtually no lending limits, so high-value homes get more liquidity.
- The Cash Account Advantage Plan is not as widely available as other reverse mortgages.
- The only payment options are a lump sum and a growing line of credit.
- Withdrawals from the line of credit must be at least $500.

- There is no mortgage insurance premium, and origination fees and closing costs can be waived with large initial withdrawals.
- The equity choice feature can help preserve equity at loan maturity.
- The adjustable interest rate is based on the six-month LIBOR index.

In sum, the Financial Freedom Cash Account Advantage Plan is primarily designed for homes worth more than $450,000. To find out more about Financial Freedom and its reverse mortgage options, call (888) 738-3773 or visit the company's Web site at *www.financialfreedom.com.*

Part III

Personal Planning

CHAPTER 6

Health Care, Long-Term Care, and Government Benefits

> *My doctor gave me six months to live, but when*
> *I couldn't pay the bill he gave me six months more.*

—Walter Matthau

Why are we devoting a chapter to health care, long-term care insurance, and government benefits in a book about reverse mortgages? By far, the biggest reported use of reverse mortgage funds is for health-care costs. Many people do not realize until it is too late just how much they will have to pay out of pocket for health-care costs as they age. The reality is that many health-care costs, and especially long-term care costs, are paid out of pocket by individuals rather than by government programs or private insurance. Another reason to discuss government benefits is that for low-income seniors who are dependent on Medicaid and Supplemental Security Income, or for those who plan to use these benefits, receiving funds from a reverse mortgage may impact eligibility for the programs.

Long-Term Care

Long-term care refers to a range of medical and social services needed to help those living with chronic health problems. It is different from acute care, which refers to short-term medical services that treat a certain illness or condition. Long-term care is provided by a variety of physicians, counselors, therapists, and nurses, and can be performed primarily in the person's home, in a nursing home, or assisted living facility. Part of the care may include assisting individuals with activities of daily living, such as dressing, bathing, eating, mobility, housekeeping, and continence. It may also include nursing care, physical therapy, caregiver training, and even hospice care.

There are many levels of long-term care, but one thing is pretty standard: from assisting daily imperative activities such as dressing and eating to helping around the house or running errands, long-term care is usually very expensive.

The cost of care can quickly deplete retirement savings and lead to Medicaid dependence and a nursing home. Most people would rather live independently in their own home than in an assisted living facility, but that can only occur if they can afford in-home care. A 2005 AARP (American Association of Retired Persons) Public Policy Institute study estimated that the average cost to maintain a disabled older person at home throughout the entire course of disability was about $174,000; the average monthly costs ran about $2,924. It is easy to see why paying out-of-pocket costs for long-term care quickly depletes many people's assets.

Who Will Need Long-Term Care?

Most Americans respond "not me" when asked if they will need long-term care services. Ironically, these same people think that everyone else will need some type of long-term care. Summary results of the 2004 National Health Interview Survey show that reality is much different from perception when it comes to health:

- Almost one-third of adults aged 75 years and over had fair or poor health.
- Sixteen percent of adults aged 45–64 years were limited in their usual activities due to one or more chronic health conditions.

- Forty-four percent of adults aged 75 years and over were limited in their usual activities due to one or more chronic health conditions.
- Ten percent of adults aged 75 years and over require the help of another person with activities of daily living (ADLs).
- Nineteen percent of adults aged 75 years and over require the help of another person with what are called instrumental ADLs, such as shopping for groceries and meal preparation.

The reality is that most of us are going to require long-term care services at some point during our life. And we know the cost of these services is high. So, the critical question is, how are we going to pay for this care?

Long-Term Care Insurance

In addition to deceiving ourselves about the need for long-term care, many people assume that they are covered by long-term care insurance. However, long-term care insurance is not part of a typical health insurance package offered by employers. Even those who do have long-term care insurance may be mistaken as to what the policy actually covers. Long-term care insurance policies differ in the type of illnesses that are covered, where policyholders can receive covered services, and when the benefits begin.

Many standard policies are focused on more extreme illnesses, during which the person needs help with major activities of daily living, such as bathing or dressing, or has a severe cognitive impairment. People who need more moderate help, such as errand-running, often rely on spouses, family, or friends to provide assistance, or they may need to move to an assisted living facility to receive help.

In addition, most policies usually define the settings in which one can receive care (nursing homes, assisted living facilities, or at home) and set dollar limits on the total amount of money the policy covers as well as the amount allowed per day or per month.

For example, many policies pay a reduced benefit for home-care costs; some pay up to 50 percent less per day for home care than for the same care provided in a nursing home.

Finally, most policies include a waiting period for coverage. For example, the policy will not begin paying for services until the policyholder has needed assistance with two or more activities of daily living for a period of ninety days. The policyholder is responsible for the costs during the first ninety days.

As you can see, you need to understand the terms of a policy in detail to know if it has value to you. Finding a policy that covers the kind of mid-level long-term care most people need is difficult. Policies with higher premiums may provide more flexible benefits, so this is definitely a case in which the fine print matters.

Using a Reverse Mortgage to Fund Long-Term Care Insurance

Perhaps due in part to people's recognition that they will be responsible for many of their own long-term care costs, the number of people purchasing long-term care policies has grown dramatically. A study by America's Health Insurance Plans, a national association representing nearly 1,300 health insurance companies, found that in 2002 more than 900,000 policies were sold, the largest number sold in a single year since 1987, when the market was first analyzed. The study also found that consumers were receiving better values for their premium dollars given that the insurance products were more consumer-driven and premiums remained largely unchanged.

If you are not covered by a long-term care insurance policy but think you should join the ranks of people who are covered, you may consider using a reverse mortgage to pay for the policy. To encourage people to purchase long-term care insurance, Congress decided to waive the HECM up-front mortgage insurance premium (MIP) for homeowners who use the entire available loan amount to purchase a qualified long-term care insurance policy.

At the time that this book was written, most analysts advised against taking out a reverse mortgage for the sole purpose of purchasing a long-term care policy. A report by The Retirement Security Project that studied this issue identified a conflict between the timing of buying long-term care insurance and getting a reverse mortgage.

It is generally better to purchase a long-term care policy at a young age, because premiums increase with age. Research by America's Health Insurance Plans found the average age of policy purchasers in 2002 to be 60 years. The average annual base premium for top long-term care insurance sellers in 2002 was $564 at 50 years, $1,337 at 65 years, and $5,330 at 79 years. In addition to paying higher premiums, those who wait too long to purchase a policy may find that they are medically ineligible.

On the other hand, people cannot even qualify for a reverse mortgage until they are at least 62 years old, and reverse mortgages tend to provide higher available loan amounts to older borrowers. Many analysts feel that the optimal age for a reverse mortgage is 72 to 75 years. Finally, older borrowers usually pay less interest expense for reverse mortgages, since the term of the loan will usually be shorter.

Another issue highlighted by The Retirement Security Project paper is that the current target markets for reverse mortgages and long-term care insurance are different. Reverse mortgages have been targeted toward lower-income persons with few assets other than their home, whereas long-term care insurance is targeted at middle- to upper-income households with a variety of assets. Indeed, at $5,000 and up for annual premiums, these policies are beyond reach for many seniors living on a tight Social Security budget.

If a low-income person with only the equity in his or her home spends all that equity on long-term care insurance, only to run out of cash before really needing the long-term care, the planning will have failed. A middle- to upper-income person with assets other than home equity may not run the same risk. Such a person may be able to use a source of funds that is less expensive than a reverse mortgage to pay the premiums.

For these reasons, the AARP and others have cautioned potential borrowers against taking out a reverse mortgage for the sole purpose of purchasing a long-term care policy. Even though it may not make sense right now to use reverse mortgage proceeds to purchase long-term care insurance, it may be wise to purchase the insurance through other means. If staying at home is your goal, just be sure the policy has a significant home-care benefit. Combining home-care benefits with a reverse mortgage may be the secret to aging at home for many middle-income households.

But what about households of more modest means that cannot afford the annual premium or worry about Medicaid eligibility? In this situation, paying directly for in-home services with reverse mortgage proceeds may make the most sense. Just be sure to match the reverse mortgage payments to the monthly in-home care costs; otherwise, any excess funds may count against Medicaid eligibility.

Government Benefits

Many of us assume we will be 100 percent covered by a government health benefit as we age and begin to need more health-care services. That is not the case. In deciding whether you will need the funds available through a reverse mortgage, it is important to understand what you can really expect from Medicare, Medicaid, and Social Security. These programs should be discussed as part of the reverse mortgage counseling requirement, so it is wise to understand the terminology ahead of time. Here is a cursory review of these benefits; only a government benefit specialist can give you an idea of what to expect in your particular situation.

Medicare

Reverse mortgage proceeds do not affect Medicare eligibility, but you may want to limit what you withdraw from a reverse mortgage based on how much of your health-care costs will be covered by Medicare and how much you will need to pay out of pocket. People 65 and over qualify for Medicare; if you receive Social Security payments and are over 65, you should automatically be enrolled.

There are two federal trust funds under the Medicare program that provide benefits. One is the Hospital Insurance (HI) Trust Fund, known as Medicare Part A, which pays for inpatient hospital and related care. Part A may cover limited stays in nursing homes. It does not cover stays in an assisted living facility, but it may cover some services provided in the facility. Although Part A is premium-free for beneficiaries who have worked and paid Medicare taxes for at least ten years, it is like private insurance programs in that there are deductibles and copayments for which the beneficiary is responsible.

The other trust fund is the Supplemental Medical Insurance (SMI) Trust Fund, which pays for physician and outpatient services under Part B and for prescription drug benefits under Part D. Part B covers 80 percent of the approved cost of a given service and 100 percent of most part-time skilled home-health care. Beneficiaries must pay a monthly premium, an annual deductible, co-insurance for the uncovered 20 percent of costs, and maybe additional charges if the health-care provider will not accept Medicare's approved payment. Also, Medicare coverage of nursing home stays is usually limited to the first one hundred days of the stay (an average stay is two and one-half years).

Medicaid

Reverse mortgage proceeds may affect Medicaid eligibility because, unlike Medicare, Medicaid is a need-based program. The Medicaid program is jointly funded by the federal government and the states. Eligibility for Medicaid varies by state, but it generally covers low-income seniors and disabled persons who meet strict asset and income limits. Most people who receive

Supplemental Security Income (federally assisted income maintenance payments) will also receive Medicaid.

Coverage also varies by state, but Medicaid pays for most out-of-pocket expenses and other services not covered by Medicare. It covers certain in-home long-term care expenses but is mainly used for nursing home stays, and longer nursing home stays than Medicare will pay for. Some states offer Medicaid home- and community-based waiver programs that cover long-term care in the home. However, most states set limits on the number of individuals who can receive waiver assistance. There are very few out-of-pocket costs for those receiving Medicaid coverage in addition to Medicare.

The concern with reverse mortgages and Medicaid is that receiving funds from a reverse mortgage may increase the beneficiary's income or assets to a level that disqualifies him or her from receiving Medicaid. The current consensus is that if the loan proceeds are spent in the month they were received, they are not considered income and will not affect benefits. However, if the funds are not spent that month, they may be counted as a resource that could lead to a termination of Medicaid benefits. Therefore, reverse mortgage borrowers who rely on Medicaid need to carefully plan and limit their withdrawals to an amount that can be spent easily each month.

Social Security

Reverse mortgage proceeds do not affect Social Security benefits, but they can be a good supplement to those benefits. You can begin drawing Social Security benefits at full retirement age, which is determined by the year you were born. For those born in 1937 or earlier, that age is 65; and for those born after 1937, the age may vary. No matter what your full retirement age, you may start drawing benefits at age 62, although the amount will be reduced if you draw early. Almost everyone over the age of 65 receives some Social Security benefit.

Supplemental Security Income

Supplemental Security Income (SSI) is a federal income supplement program designed to help people aged 65 or older, as well as people who are blind or disabled and have little or no income and few assets or resources. The program provides cash for basic needs such as food, shelter, and clothing. In 2007, the highest amount of SSI paid to an individual was $623 per month, and the highest amount paid to a couple was $934 per month. States may add money to the federal SSI payments; that amount varies by state.

The SSI amount is usually based on the person's income from the previous two months, so the amount received may be different each month. Anything a person receives that can be used to acquire food, clothing, or shelter is considered income. A home in which a person lives is not counted as a resource, and reverse mortgage proceeds are not counted as income as long as the proceeds are spent the same month they are received. If the proceeds are not spent during the month in which they were received, they will be considered a resource and could affect SSI eligibility, just as they do Medicaid eligibility.

Other Programs

The federal and state programs discussed in the previous sections are the major sources of income and assistance for seniors. Of course, there are many minor programs as well, such as state property tax deferral programs, food stamps, and supplemental food programs. Many of these programs, combined with private charities, support independent living. Although the small programs tend to be easy targets of budget cuts, it is likely that, given the high cost of nursing home care borne by governments and individuals, we will see more programs aimed at helping people remain in their homes as they age.

An AARP Public Policy Institute study found that, in the year 2000, about $102 billion was spent on long-term care and independent living for persons aged 65 and over. The report included estimates of costs for a range of activities related to long-term care and independent living, not just costs in the health-care sector. It also looked at nonresidential services, such as the services of home health-care providers; physical, occupational, and speech therapists; home-delivered and congregate meals; special needs transportation; medical equipment and supplies; and home or vehicle modifications.

The most useful part of the study for our purposes was discovering who funds these services. Almost 20 percent of overall spending on long-term care and independent living was paid for out of pocket. On top of that, these estimates do not include time and money spent by family members, friends, and neighbors, who may provide many hours of informal care to those in need. No wonder so many people are relying on reverse mortgages to cover out-of-pocket health-care costs and to compensate friends and neighbors who provide informal care.

The Future of Benefit Programs

You have probably seen a news article or program about looming shortages and deficits in Social Security, Medicare, and other government programs. Health-care costs place a heavy burden on governments, and that burden is increasing with the aging of our population. According to an article from the Centers for Medicare and Medicaid Services, about one-third of federal revenues and one-quarter of state and local governments' revenues go to health care.

And Medicare spending is growing rapidly. The 2006 Medicare Trustees Report estimated that total Medicare expenditures will be 3.2 percent of gross domestic product in 2006 and will reach 11 percent by 2080. This rapid growth is due in part to increases in health-care prices, greater-than-expected use of medical services, and increases in the severity of illnesses of patients enrolled in Medicare plans. In addition to making greater use of services, the aging of the population means that there are fewer workers to put money into these programs. In 2006, there were

3.9 workers for every beneficiary; by 2030, there will only be about 2.4 workers per beneficiary. (In 1950, there were 16.5 workers per beneficiary.)

The Trustees Report also found that by 2018 the HI Trust Fund will likely be insolvent. Competition and preventive care in all medical expense areas are viewed as key to reducing Medicare spending. Another proposal is to gradually increase the share of program costs paid by the highest-income beneficiaries.

While the SMI Trust Fund does not suffer the same funding shortages as the HI Trust Fund (it is automatically funded from general fund revenues and supplemented by monthly premiums charged to beneficiaries), the program is not immune to increasing health-care costs and claims. As the estimated costs of the programs go up, the monthly premium amounts will also increase. In fact, high-income beneficiaries will probably pay greater Part B premiums starting in 2007.

In addition to SMI premiums, beneficiaries may be responsible for Part B cost-sharing liabilities, particularly if they receive above-average medical services. Many beneficiaries use employer-sponsored retiree health plans or "Medigap" private insurance to pay for a substantial portion of Part B cost-sharing liabilities. Low-income beneficiaries usually qualify for Part D low-income subsidies and Medicaid, so they have little or no cost sharing or premium payments. Typical Medicare SMI beneficiaries, who do not receive subsidized coverage, may soon find that the growing out-of-pocket SMI costs will consume a significant portion of their income.

Comparing Social Security to Medicare, the projections for Social Security are better in the short term because costs for this program grow more slowly. Rising Social Security costs are primarily a result of longer life expectancy, whereas Medicare costs are tied to health-care costs. However, the major source of funding for Social Security is payroll taxes, so it will suffer as the number of workers per beneficiary declines. Many analysts expect to see trouble between 2010 and 2030 as the baby-boom generation retires. The 2006 Annual Report of the Social Security Board of Trustees determined that projected Social Security tax income will begin to fall short of outlays in 2017.

The primary methods of correcting this imbalance are to raise payroll taxes and reduce benefits. Other methods include using general revenue funds and private savings accounts. Most reform measures preserve full benefits (including cost-of-living increases) to current beneficiaries and near-retirees (those 55 and older).

The situation is similar for state budgets that are being consumed by health-care costs. Most states have implemented some kind of cost containment measures on Medicaid spending. Of course, one of the best ways to contain costs is to restrict eligibility and benefits.

While all of these statistics and projections can leave one with a sense of impending financial doom, the good news is that everyone recognizes the potential that reverse mortgages have to help the aging population manage health-care costs, including long-term care and long-term care insurance. We see a bright future in which private companies will innovate and offer lower-cost and more flexible products, and governments will regulate and encourage consumer-friendly products that work with, instead of against, existing government programs. Still, it is best to plan early to cover many of your own health-care costs and not depend on government benefits unless you have to.

CHAPTER 7

Alternatives to a Reverse Mortgage

> *As a child my family's menu consisted of two choices: take it or leave it.*
>
> —Buddy Hackett

Luckily, when it comes to planning for our future, we have more choices than Buddy did at mealtime. A reverse mortgage is one option for covering expenses and preserving an independent lifestyle. However, if you do not want to spend your home equity right now, there may be other ways to meet your needs. This chapter highlights several alternatives to reverse mortgages.

Alternatives to a Reverse Mortgage

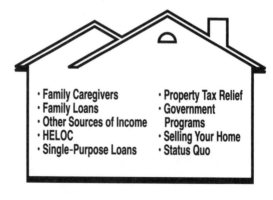

- Family Caregivers
- Family Loans
- Other Sources of Income
- HELOC
- Single-Purpose Loans
- Property Tax Relief
- Government Programs
- Selling Your Home
- Status Quo

You may decide that one of these alternatives is satisfactory, or you may have to combine a reverse mortgage with one of the alternatives to meet all of your needs.

Family Caregivers

For seniors who live near family members, an alternative to using a reverse mortgage to pay for home care and assistance may be to enlist the help of a family caregiver. Caregivers can also be close friends, neighbors, or partners. They help buy groceries, assist with personal grooming, maintain and repair homes, give medication, and manage medical appointments. Most important, they love and support people faced with chronic illness or disability. And they do so free of charge.

A March 2006 report by the AARP found that reliance upon family caregivers has been increasing while the use of paid, formal care has been decreasing. The National Family Caregivers Association (NFCA) estimates that more than 50 million people provide care for a chronically ill, disabled, or aged family member or friend in any given year. In 2003, the NFCA and Dr. Peter S. Arno conducted a state-by-state analysis of the prevalence and economic value of family caregiving. They estimated that caregivers provided approximately 29 million hours of services per year, for an annual market value of approximately $257 million.

While it is good news that the extended family is making a comeback, there are some shortcomings that need to be addressed to keep caregivers and recipients of care happy, healthy, and working together for the long haul. Studies continually show that family caregivers suffer from severe stress and stress-related illnesses. Many caregivers are still responsible for their own children or grandchildren in addition to their parents. In the balancing act of juggling everyone's needs, the caregiver's physical and emotional health are often neglected.

Because people are now living longer with chronic illnesses, today's caregivers provide care for much longer periods of time than ever before. They often experience financial hardship due to taking time off from work to provide care. In addition, many caregivers quit their jobs or retire early because they cannot manage full-time work along with caring for children, spouses, and parents.

An important step in getting help is recognizing that people who provide assistance to family members are caregivers who need education and support, just as do health-care professionals. Nonprofit groups such as the NFCA and the Family Caregiver Alliance advocate for family caregivers and encourage caregivers to take care of themselves and to reach out and get help. Some companies are starting to adopt more compassionate policies for family caregivers, such as flexible hours, telecommuting, and eldercare support services.

Another way to lessen the stress for family caregivers may be to use the proceeds from a reverse mortgage to provide them with cash assistance. This is really helpful if the caregiver is missing work and taking a cut in pay or providing transportation or running errands. In such a case, providing the family member with money for gasoline may make both parties feel more comfortable with the assistance. Using reverse mortgage proceeds may also be helpful if the person needing care is rejecting help from a family member because of pride or worries about being a burden. Beyond that, the proceeds can be used to supplement family caregiving with commercial in-home care services.

Family Loans

Before lending qualifications became as relaxed as they are today, many people relied on family members for loans. This may still be a good option today, as long as the transaction is carefully documented and all family members agree to and understand the terms. It is never wise to compromise family relationships over money, so the emotional side effects of this option need to be considered carefully. Since there are minimal fees and no lending limits in a private transaction, investing in an attorney to document the transaction is a good idea.

For example, two clients, a husband and wife in their mid-80s, felt they would not live long enough to justify the fees of a commercial reverse mortgage. Instead, their daughter agreed to lend them money for living expenses via a loan that resembled a reverse mortgage. The clients and all their children discussed this family loan and agreed it was the best solution. The loan was established to provide monthly payments to the parents. Just like a third-party reverse mortgage, the daughter had a deed of trust filed on the property and obtained a lender's title policy. Everyone was happy at the end of process, and the family saved quite a bit of money on loan costs. Documenting a reverse-like mortgage between private parties is more complicated than a forward mortgage, so be sure to work with a qualified attorney.

Investments and Other Sources of Income

Investments provide opportunities to receive cash disbursements like those from a reverse mortgage. One regularly advertised retirement investment is an annuity. An annuity is a long-term financial investment that can provide a source of income during retirement. You can choose annuities that make payments on a monthly, quarterly, or annual basis. Some annuities begin making payments as soon as you invest; others start payments later. You can purchase one by paying for the entire annuity at once in a lump sum payment, or you can choose a more flexible plan that allows for ongoing contributions.

As with reverse mortgages, research the fees and compare the costs and benefits of the various annuity products to decide whether these products are right for you. Other types of investments (for example, stocks, bonds, or mutual funds) may provide a better return once you factor in the cost of the annuity. In most cases it will not make sense to use money from a reverse mortgage to purchase an annuity. The high costs and debt from the combined products will not outweigh the income you will receive. It is best to view reverse mortgages and annuities as alternatives or congruent sources of income.

If you only need a small amount of extra cash to meet monthly expenses, you may want to consider these options:

- Rent out a spare bedroom or the basement in your home.
- Get a part-time job.
- Sell homemade items or antiques and collectibles at a consignment shop, farmer's market, or craft bazaar.
- Start a home-based business.

If you do not mind the company, renting out a spare bedroom or the basement is a good way to earn extra income. Renting is safest if you can share your home with a friend or family member. If you take in a stranger, get as many references as possible and follow through by contacting the references. The United Way sponsors several Senior Services Homesharing Programs around the country. This is an intergenerational program that matches homeowners and renters. One person in the match must be 55 years of age or older, and all parties undergo a background check and provide references.

One of our grandfathers had many postretirement business adventures, including buying, repairing, and selling old sewing machines. This combined his enjoyment of fixing things with the needs of his community, and made money for him. He lives near an Amish community, where there is high demand for refurbished sewing machines that can be converted to treadle power. Look around your neighborhood and think about hobbies or tasks that you enjoy; there may be a need for your services.

If you need a large amount of cash all at once, consider selling high-price assets. For example, sell the boat that sits in the driveway under a tarp all year round. The same applies to recreational vehicles, extra cars, or a vacation home.

Home Equity Line of Credit

If you have enough income to qualify for a home equity line of credit (HELOC), you may want to consider this instead of a reverse mortgage. As its name implies, it is set up as a line of credit that you can draw upon at any time up to the maximum approved amount. While a HELOC has lower up-front costs than does a reverse mortgage, the interest rate risk is higher because there are normally no adjustment caps. Some HELOCs have a guaranteed introductory rate, but this introductory rate typically lasts only a few months. Unlike a reverse mortgage, a HELOC must be repaid on a monthly basis. If you can afford the payments, a HELOC can cover large expenses without drawing down your home equity.

For example, suppose you turn 62 and the roof starts leaking on the home you have lived in for the past thirty years. You are still working and can afford a small monthly payment because you paid off your forward mortgage last year. So, instead of using a reverse mortgage, you take out a $7,500 home equity line of credit to pay for a new roof and aim to pay it off in the three to five years before you retire. The roof is repaired and your home equity is preserved for later use when you stop working and have another large expense.

Single-Purpose Loans

Another alternative to a reverse mortgage for covering extraordinary expenses is a single-purpose loan. Single-purpose loans are offered by many state and local governments and nonprofit organizations to help seniors cover home repair and property expenses. These loans are like reverse mortgages in that repayment is often deferred; they do not need to be repaid as long as you live in the home. They differ from reverse mortgages since the proceeds from the loan must be used for a specific purpose—home repairs—not anything you wish. The costs and fees for these loans are usually much lower than for reverse mortgages, and under some programs the loan may be forgiven if you continue to live in your home for a certain number of years. So, a single-purpose loan is a good choice if all you need is money for an expensive home repair such as replacing an old furnace or leaky roof.

Single-purpose loans that do not require repayment as long as you live in the home are referred to as deferred payment loans (DPL). Eligibility for DPLs is normally limited to homeowners with incomes far below the median income for a given area; more than 50 percent below for some programs. DPLs are typically low-cost loans with low interest rates; there are no origination fees or mortgage insurance. Needless to say, a DPL is a much better choice than a HELOC for those who meet the low-income qualifications.

One widely available DPL offered by the federal government is the Rural Housing Repair and Rehabilitation Loan offered through the U.S. Department of Agriculture Rural Development office. These loans are for low-income rural homeowners age 62 and older who are unable to get credit elsewhere. Low income means very low: 50 percent below the area's median income. Loans of up to $20,000 and grants (which do not have to be repaid) of up to $7,500 are available to make a home safer or more sanitary or to remove health and safety hazards. Given the low lending limits for rural properties imposed by typical reverse mortgages, DPLs such as this one are a vital safety net for rural homeowners.

There also are two states—Connecticut and Montana—that offer single-purpose loans that provide income payments, like a reverse mortgage.

Typical Single-Purpose Loans

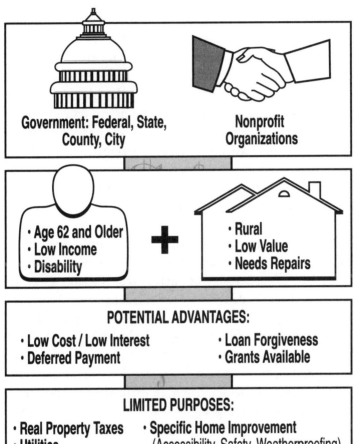

Government: Federal, State, County, City

Nonprofit Organizations

- Age 62 and Older
- Low Income
- Disability

+

- Rural
- Low Value
- Needs Repairs

POTENTIAL ADVANTAGES:

- Low Cost / Low Interest
- Deferred Payment
- Loan Forgiveness
- Grants Available

LIMITED PURPOSES:

- Real Property Taxes
- Utilities
- Specific Home Improvement (Accessibility, Safety, Weatherproofing)

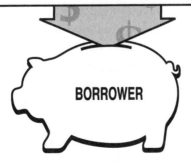

BORROWER

Property Tax Relief Programs

The housing bubble has made homes worth more, which is good if you are selling your home but not so good if you are staying put and paying property taxes. Escalating property taxes are particularly hard for seniors whose incomes are stagnant or declining. Many states and municipalities offer some type of assistance to seniors, veterans, and disabled persons who have difficulty paying property taxes. Some of the programs are restricted to low-income seniors; others are available to all seniors. There are three main types of property tax assistance programs:

- Property tax abatement programs
- Homestead exemption or tax credit programs
- Property tax deferral programs

Under abatement programs, states or municipalities may reduce or waive property taxes for qualifying seniors. Abatements are often based on hardship but may also be available for property located in historic districts or revitalization areas. Some counties offer property tax work-off abatement programs that help seniors with taxes while tapping their knowledge and skills for the community. These programs require seniors to work a minimum number of hours at a designated job assignment, such as the town library or senior center, in exchange for a tax write-off equal to their earned wages.

Homestead exemption and tax credit programs reduce the amount of assessed property value subject to taxation. For example, Colorado's Senior Homestead Exemption Program reduces the property tax on primary residences by exempting 50 percent of the first $200,000 in market value. If your residence is worth $200,000, $100,000 will be exempt from taxation. To qualify, seniors must be at least 65 years old as of January 1 in the year the application is made and have owned and lived in the property as a primary residence for at least ten consecutive years prior to January 1. Other exemption programs freeze the assessed value of the home, and still others exclude home improvements from the assessed value for a number of years after the improvement. "Circuit breaker" programs provide grants or rebates to seniors who are overloaded by high property taxes.

Property tax deferral programs allow seniors to postpone payment of their property taxes until they die or sell the property. They are really a type of single-purpose or deferred payment loan. The state pays the property taxes for the homeowner, charges interest each year on the unpaid amount (often 5–6 percent), and takes a lien on the property to secure repayment upon death or sale of the property. The total amount of tax deferred usually cannot exceed a percentage of the homeowner's equity in the property (often 80–85 percent). Once the limit is reached, the homeowner is once again responsible for paying the taxes at the time they are due.

Whether you receive an abatement, exemption, credit, or deferral, most programs require you to reapply for the assistance each tax year to confirm that you still meet the eligibility requirements. Given the importance of tax revenue to government budgets and the limited amount of assistance available, government officials want to make sure that only those who really need the help are using the program's resources. So, make sure you track and meet the application deadlines each year.

Another option for reducing property taxes is to challenge the assessment of your property's value. The process is fairly simple, and most homeowners can do it themselves. You will need to meet the protest deadline, follow the assessor's procedures, and gather evidence. Assessments can be challenged if you feel there was a mistake in the assessment of your home or if your home was assessed at a higher rate than comparable homes. You should at least review the assessment each year to make sure information about your home, such as square footage and number of bedrooms, is correct.

Probably the most difficult part of obtaining a single-purpose loan or property tax relief is finding out how to apply. Most of these programs are not widely advertised. That is probably because each program is unique and may change from year to year based on state and local funding limits. Also, some programs may be limited to a certain number of participants. Check with your state department of revenue or county assessor's office for more information on eligibility and application deadlines. Your local Area Agency on Aging, discussed in the next section, may also have information about these programs.

Government Assistance

Area Agencies on Aging (AAA) are a comprehensive resource for senior services and programs. AAAs were established under the Older Americans Act in 1973 to develop and implement a wide array of home and community services for Americans aged 60 and over. The Older Americans Act also set up Title VI agencies to serve the unique needs of aging Native Americans, Aleuts, Eskimos, and Hawaiians. In 2000, the Older Americans Act was amended to include the National Family Caregiver Support Program, which provides grants to states to fund AAA programs aimed at helping family members who care for seniors. The following broad categories of services are available through AAAs and Title VI agencies:

- Information and access services (for example, Medicare and Medicaid counseling and transportation to critical destinations)
- Community-based services (for example, senior centers and adult day care)
- In-home services (for example, Meals on Wheels and housekeeping)
- Housing services (for example, senior housing and assisted living facilities)
- Elder rights services (for example, legal assistance and elder abuse prevention programs)

For seniors who have low incomes and few assets, it makes good sense to check with the local Area Agency on Aging before taking out a reverse mortgage to see if there are other options for covering day-to-day expenses such as meals and transportation. The agency may be able to find a program or service to cover those costs so that home equity can be reserved for later unexpected expenses. In addition, since the mission of AAAs and Title VI agencies is to help seniors live independently, these agencies are a good first stop for questions about long-term care options and expenses.

Like other government programs that assist with health and aging issues, AAAs and Title VI agencies are challenged by funding constraints and the growing population of individuals eligible for their services. Many agencies have growing waiting lists for services. AAAs are tackling these challenges by maximizing private and public resources. It is a good idea to contact them earlier rather than later.

One final idea to consider for seniors struggling with expenses is utility assistance. As the price of gas, electricity, and water continues to rise, many people are struggling to pay their utility bills. This is especially a problem in the winter and summer months, when heating and cooling costs tend to be higher. Many utility companies offer payment plans to seniors that spread the utility costs evenly over the year or even reduce the payments. In fact, some utility companies offer everyone (not just seniors) rebates or credits for installing certain energy-saving products and completing energy-saving remodeling.

The key to finding a program that fits your needs is to keep looking and asking questions. Inevitably, the first person you talk to will not have all the answers. Also, keep in mind that if the money you receive from one of these programs results in a lien on your house, you will not be able to receive a reverse mortgage until it is repaid. The bottom line is that you need to be sure you can still take out a reverse mortgage if you participate in one of these programs.

Selling the Home

One of the biggest questions you have to answer when considering a reverse mortgage is "Do you want to stay in your home?" If remaining in your home is not a priority for you, it may make sense to sell and relocate. Things to consider when deciding whether to stay put or move include:

- The money you may receive from selling your home (sales price minus existing mortgage and costs)
- Maintenance and upkeep for your current home
- Proximity to family and friends
- The availability of health care and senior services
- The availability of cultural and recreational activities
- The cost of living in a different home or community, including the cost of property taxes and the availability of property tax relief programs

Selling your home does not always mean you have to relocate to a new home. It is possible to sell your home and retain the right to live in it for the rest of your life (a life estate) or rent it back from the buyer. These scenarios often work best when the buyer is a trusted family member or close friend. The buyer receives the benefit of the home's appreciation, and you pay a nominal rental fee. Some financial institutions offer sales leaseback programs.

Under the right circumstances it may make sense to sell your home and use the proceeds to fund a charitable remainder trust. However, this is a complex estate-planning technique and is normally only used by wealthy individuals. With a charitable remainder trust, the proceeds from the sale of your home are invested through a trust, and you receive, for life, a portion of the investment income that is generated. This also allows the homeowner to take a current tax deduction when the home is sold. At death, the remaining investment is given to a previously designated charity.

If you decide to sell and relocate, there are many places to make a new home:

- A house, modular home, condominium, or townhouse
- A manufactured home or RV
- A family member's home
- A rental house, apartment, or room
- An assisted living facility or senior community

There are also many loan programs that can help with relocation costs. Fannie Mae offers a HomeChoice mortgage program for family members who need to remodel their home to accommodate aging parents with disabilities. Refer back to Chapter 4 for more about the Fannie Mae Home Keeper for Home Purchase loan (a type of reverse mortgage for purchasing a new home).

Status Quo

Not making a decision is itself a decision. After reading this book and consulting with your advisers, you may decide to do nothing. Recognize that this is a choice. It may be a good choice if you determine you don't need additional funds or assistance at this time or if you need more information. On the other hand, if you know that you need additional funds to accomplish your retirement goals but you are still not sure of the value that a reverse mortgage could have for you, turn to the next chapter to find out.

CHAPTER 8

What Is a Reverse Mortgage Worth to Me?

> *Price is what you pay. Value is what you get.*
>
> —Warren Buffet

Buffet's wisdom is especially true for reverse mortgages. The value of a reverse mortgage includes much more than the price. You may be willing to pay a high price to get the financial security and peace of mind that comes with a reverse mortgage. On the other hand, if a reverse mortgage does not fit into your retirement plan or will not provide a unique benefit, you may not be able to justify the price.

How do you determine the value that a reverse mortgage could have for you? Start by learning all you can about reverse mortgages. Next, identify your goals and compare them to the pros and cons of a reverse mortgage. Throughout the learning process, be sure you ask lots of questions. Asking the right questions dramatically increases your chance of making the right decision. This chapter includes plenty of the right questions. It also offers factors to consider when developing your personal and financial retirement plan.

Your Retirement Expectations and Goals

> *How am I going to live today in order to create the tomorrow I'm committed to?*
>
> —Anthony Robbins

The first step to establishing a balanced retirement plan is to take a close look at your retirement goals. Goals regarding where you want to live, the legacy you will leave when you are gone, and your desired retirement lifestyle will influence your thinking about reverse mortgages. For simplicity, these goals can be categorized into three general areas: liberty, legacy, and lifestyle (the three Ls).

Retirement Goals

Liberty   Legacy
Lifestyle

Liberty

Americans value independence, but we also cherish our communities. It isn't surprising that as we age, many of our biggest concerns are related to financial independence and autonomous living. These are some questions to ask yourself to gauge your attitude toward independent living:

- What type of living arrangements do I prefer (alone, with another person, in a group)?

- If I develop a chronic illness or disability, does that change my living arrangement preference?
- Do I want to stay in my home, or move to a new home?
- How important is being in a community with family and friends?
- Do I prefer to set my own schedule, or do I like scheduled activities?
- Am I comfortable relying on government benefits?
- Am I comfortable with financial help from family and friends?
- Do I want to continue working in some capacity as I age?

It appears that most Americans prefer to remain in their existing homes as they age, even if that means living alone. According to the 2000 U.S. Census, only about 6 percent of people 65 and older lived in group quarters; the rest lived alone or with others in a household. Similarly, a 2004 study by the MetLife Mature Market Institute and AARP Health Care Options found that 86 percent of pre-retirees prefer to continue living in their own home during retirement if they are able to live without ongoing assistance, and 49 percent prefer to do so even if they need day-to-day assistance or ongoing health care.

In addition to living independently, we value financial independence. The reality, however, is that many Americans have not saved enough money to maintain that independence as they age. In surveys, baby-boomers (the generation born from 1943 to 1960) admit that they have not thought much about retirement and are not financially prepared for it. Many of them plan to work past the traditional retirement age, but they will likely live longer as well, so the additional years of earnings may not help that much once they do retire.

The U.S. Census Bureau reports that in 1999, the average annual Social Security income to the 90 percent of households with persons 65 and older who receive Social Security was $12,300. For those who had sources of income other than Social

Security, that retirement income averaged $17,900 per year. While this may cover basic living expenses, it does not provide much cushion for unexpected expenses. A combination of Social Security and a reverse mortgage may be the only way to pay bills and extraordinary expenses without relying on financial assistance from family or other sources.

Legacy

A concern about whether there will be anything left for heirs is one of the main reasons people reject reverse mortgages. People want to leave something for their children, and for most of us, home equity represents one-half or more of the entire estate. A reverse mortgage does deplete that home equity, but it does not necessarily mean there will be no equity to pass on to children or heirs.

There are ways to use a reverse mortgage and preserve home equity for your estate. If the home continues to appreciate and the loan balance remains below the market value of the house, it is likely that when the house is sold there will be cash remaining to distribute to heirs. Instead of relying on market forces for appreciation, be proactive and set aside a portion of your principal limit that will not be accessed. The Cash Account Advantage Plan reverse mortgage from Financial Freedom does this for you through its equity choice feature, but you can mimic this feature with any reverse mortgage through a sound financial plan and self-discipline.

Keep in mind that a legacy includes everything that you leave to your heirs including values, memories, inheritance, heirlooms, and family history, not just wealth. Today, people place less emphasis on leaving money to their heirs. Perhaps it is because we have seen too many bad examples of children receiving large sums of money from their parents only to become dysfunctional and unproductive. Sandy Kraemer, an estate-planning attorney and writer on the topic of inheritance, refers to this unfortunate scenario as "intergenerational retrogression."

If you are not going to leave much money to your heirs but want some sort of legacy, think about what things other than money to leave your heirs. For example, draw a detailed family tree or write a journal of family stories. Better yet, film yourself telling family stories and leave a copy of the DVD for each child and grandchild. Or, set aside a family heirloom (for example, Grandmother's teapot or your prized golf clubs) for each child, with an explanation of its history. These gifts take effort to make but will mean more to your family than money. Most adult children would rather see their parents use their home equity to take care of themselves than struggle to save to create an inheritance.

Regardless of the size of your estate, be sure you have a current estate plan. An estate plan normally includes a will or trust, a financial and medical power of attorney, and a living will (sometimes called a medical directive). As circumstances change, be sure to have your estate plan updated. Changes in circumstances may include a financial change or death of a spouse or other family member. One sure-fire way to leave a legacy you will not be proud of is to die without an estate plan. Children and beneficiaries can bicker over $10,000 just as much as they can bicker over $500,000. Leaving your estate to be sorted out by your beneficiaries and the default probate laws of your state results only in disputes and unnecessary expenses. Be proud that your guidance will be needed even after you are gone; give it now.

Lifestyle

Lifestyle is the way a person lives. Lifestyles can be based on geography, religious affiliations, social issues, occupations, and a number of other habits and preferences. Some common lifestyle dichotomies we hear about are rural versus urban, sedentary versus recreational, military versus civilian, and simple living versus conspicuous consumption.

Aging can be stressful because changes and threats to our current lifestyle may require us to adapt to a new lifestyle. In 2001 and 2005, the MetLife Mature Market Institute conducted surveys of baby-boomers' attitudes toward retirement. In the 2001 study, boomers were optimistic about retirement, but by 2005 the number who said they were worried about retirement doubled. The study tied this worry to increasing concerns about financial independence and declining lifestyles during retirement. If preserving or improving your lifestyle is important to you, a reverse mortgage may be a means to do so.

To determine your retirement lifestyle, start by making a detailed list of goals for your retirement years. Defining your goals will help you identify how you want to live so that you can plan to accomplish that lifestyle. It may also reduce feelings of disorientation, depression, and frustration that sometimes accompany retirement. Creating goals prepares people for change, and being mentally prepared is as important as being financially prepared when it comes to the retirement years. These are some questions that will help you define your desired retirement lifestyle:

- Am I content to cover basic needs?
- Are there any luxuries that I can do without as I age?
- Are there luxuries that I will want when I age that I do not have now?
- Do I want my postretirement lifestyle to be the same as or different from my current lifestyle? If different, then how so?
- Do I plan to travel, take on a new hobby, or dedicate myself to a charitable cause?
- Am I going to exercise and work hard to stay healthy?
- Do I have a medical condition that will impact my lifestyle if it worsens?
- What are the biggest risks to my lifestyle?
- Can I cover large, unexpected expenses without compromising my lifestyle?

In order to know what financial resources you will need to support your expected lifestyle, you should create an estimated retirement budget and make sure you really understand your current and future financial situation.

Your Retirement Budget

Perhaps you feel secure about retirement based on income you expect to receive from pensions, investments, or Social Security. Or maybe you worry that unexpected health-care costs will quickly deplete your limited savings. Whether you feel confident or anxious, move beyond your feelings for a moment and look at the numbers.

If you are not good with numbers or question your objectivity, you may want to seek help with your financial plan. Hire an accountant or financial planner or ask a family member or friend to help create a budget and financial statement. There are also many user-friendly software programs, such as Intuit Quicken and Microsoft Money, that can help you manage and understand your finances. Some software programs, especially those used in-house by financial planners, may even include a reverse mortgage analysis tool.

A basic financial review usually covers income and expenses in a cash-flow worksheet, and assets and liabilities in a financial statement. The first and most important step in looking at cash flow is to make sure you can cover expenses for basic needs such as food, shelter, utilities, and medicines. The next step is to identify other actual expenses, such as credit card and debt payments, taxes, and insurance. Finally, consider wants or nonessential expenses, such as gifts for grandchildren, vacations, or contributions to a savings or investment account.

Expenses usually decrease during early retirement for several reasons. First, contributions to savings and investments slow down or stop altogether. Second, work-related expenses, including travel, meals away from home, business clothing, and business entertainment, disappear. Third, there are many discounts available to seniors. Fourth, mortgage payments at this point are low or nonexistent.

One widely used method of roughly estimating retirement living expenses, especially for those close to retirement or already retired, is this formula: Estimated retirement spending = (Current gross annual income – amount of annual savings) × 75 percent. To use this formula to create a projection of the necessary retirement income at the anticipated retirement age, the result must be adjusted for inflation.

For example, if Barry plans to retire in seven years and has a current annual income of $95,000, of which he saves $16,000 per year, he would need $59,250 of annual retirement income in today's dollars to cover his estimated expenses ($95,000 – $16,000 × .75). If we assume 3 percent annual inflation each year for seven years until retirement, he will need an annual retirement income of approximately $72,900 to cover expenses.

Think broadly but conservatively on the income side of the financial statement. Income can derive from a variety of sources, such as a job, Social Security, pensions, retirement savings, and annuities or other investments that pay dividends or interest. Make sure you understand the timing of, and any restrictions on, income-producing assets. For example, if you cash in a 1-year CD (certificate of deposit) before it matures, you will pay a penalty.

Retirement planning also needs to consider risks and identify safeguards. For example, what happens if you outlive your retirement assets? Planning based on an average life expectancy may grossly underestimate your needs. Today, the possibility of living until age 95 is not unrealistic. We have a great-grandmother who recently celebrated her 106th birthday. Our incredulity at this event was dimmed when the nursing home informed us that they had eight centenarians in their facility. She supported herself at home until she was 102 years old.

Americans are not only living longer but are also retiring earlier in some cases. The extended retirement phase of life takes diligent planning. We have an aunt who retired at age 55, but she is one of the fortunate Santa Barbara homeowners. Even with a high-value home to cash out, she has to rely on other investments and sources of income to sustain her extended retirement. She also realizes that going back to work, either part-time or through her own business, may be necessary at some point.

A big risk in retirement planning is health care. Greater medical expenses are a distinct possibility during retirement, and they are difficult to budget. It goes without saying that regular exercise, proper diet, and regular status visits to your doctor are a great way to maximize your quality of life during retirement and decrease possible medical costs. It is also important to understand your health insurance plan and become familiar with the Medicare program, including the need for Medicare gap insurance. Early retirees will also have to budget for the cost of maintaining their health insurance policy before they become eligible for Medicare.

There are various risks that may affect retirement security:
- Outliving retirement assets
- Developing a chronic illness or disability that limits working during retirement
- Overestimating income from pensions, investments, or Social Security
- Higher than expected out-of-pocket health-care costs
- Unanticipated expenses, such as major home repairs or necessary home accommodations for disabilities
- Economic changes such as inflation, stock market downturns, and energy prices

Many people fail to appreciate the impact of inflation in planning for retirement. If you live primarily on fixed annuities or interest, inflation will decrease the buying power of your income over time. Fixed reverse mortgage payments are also subject to the adverse affects of inflation. A line of credit that earns interest is the best way to reduce or even eliminate the effects of inflation on a reverse mortgage. Continuing to own your home offers inflation protection because home prices usually increase with inflation.

A helpful calculation for understanding the impact of inflation is the rule of 72. Take the number 72 and divide it by the average rate of inflation to determine the number of years that it will take for the buying power of today's dollar to be cut in half. For example, if the rate of inflation is 3 percent, an item that costs $10 today will cost $20 in 24 years (72 ÷ 3 = 24).

With the prospect of a longer retirement and the impact of inflation on retirement income, you need to consider the rate at which you make withdrawals from retirement accounts. If too much is withdrawn, you may have to cut back later and may even run out of savings. The same consideration also applies to withdrawals from a reverse mortgage line of credit or monthly payment plan.

Several groups have studied what a sustainable withdrawal rate might be for a retired senior. Assuming a reasonable rate of return for a reasonably diversified portfolio (6 percent to 8 percent), a withdrawal rate of 5 percent to 6 percent should be sustainable for about thirty years. Those who plan to retire early or have longer life expectancies may be better off with a 3 percent to 4 percent withdrawal rate. A financial planner or CPA can help you determine a withdrawal rate that fits your situation.

The Top 10 Reverse Mortgage Questions

Asking the right questions helps you discover the right answers and make the right decisions. This chapter has asked questions to get you thinking about retirement expectations and financial planning. Following is a list of ten practical questions that summarize the knowledge of reverse mortgages that you have gained from the previous chapters. Before proceeding with a reverse mortgage, ask yourself:

1. Am I the right age to get a reverse mortgage?
2. Is this home my primary residence?
3. How much equity do I have in my home?
4. How much money should I take from a reverse mortgage?
5. Will I want or need to move from my home in the near future?

6. Do I expect to receive any low-income assistance?
7. Do I have a well-balanced retirement plan and a clear reason for getting a reverse mortgage?
8. Do I understand how a reverse mortgage works and how it will fit into my personal plans?
9. Have I considered my alternatives?
10. Am I willing to reduce the inheritance that may one day go to my children?

Number 1: Am I the right age to get a reverse mortgage?

As you have probably memorized by now, the primary qualification for a reverse mortgage is that each borrower must be 62 or older and that the age of the youngest borrower is the age used to determine the available loan amount. Most people feel that the age bracket most well suited to a reverse mortgage is the mid-70s. At that age, you are old enough to receive a high loan amount and young enough that the term of the loan will be long enough to justify the costs.

Number 2: Is this home my primary residence?

It is easy for most of us to determine whether a property is our primary residence; there is only one choice. It can get tricky if you own a vacation home, especially if you plan to spend six months or more in the vacation home each year. According to a National Association of Realtors survey, one-quarter of baby-boomers own one or more kinds of real estate in addition to a primary residence. Four out of ten respondents said they plan to convert their vacation home into a primary residence when they retire. These questions are often used to establish a person's primary residence: Where do you pay state income taxes? Where do you vote? Where is your car registered?

Number 3: How much equity do I have in my home?

Equity is the market value of your house minus any existing mortgage debt and other liens encumbering your house. There are a number of online tools to help you get an idea of the market value of your house. One popular Web site is *www.zillow.com;* it provides a free estimate of your home value based on recent sales of other homes in your area. You can also check the newspaper for the asking prices of houses for sale in your neighborhood. These methods are not perfect but should give you a sense of the market value of your house. You can estimate your equity by deducting the amount of any existing debt from the market value. As a rule of thumb, you can expect to be able to convert between 35 percent and 70 percent of your home equity into cash with a reverse mortgage.

Number 4: How much money should I take from a reverse mortgage?

This is where reverse mortgages get complicated, because they tie into both present and future financial planning. If you take out a reverse mortgage because of an immediate need (for example, a new roof), then you should limit yourself to withdrawing enough to cover that need and save the rest for later. If you are doing it to cover monthly expenses, the payments should be matched to your monthly budget. A good counselor, lender, or financial planner can help you determine how much to take now and how much to save for unexpected expenses.

Number 5: Will I want or need to move from my home in the near future?

Moving will trigger repayment of a reverse mortgage. Remember from our discussion of reverse mortgage costs in Chapter 2 that it is best if you can plan to stay in your home for several years after taking out a reverse mortgage. This allows you to spread the high cost of the loan over a longer period of time, thereby reducing the impact of the costs. Most industry experts agree you should plan to stay in your home for at least three to five years; some believe it takes seven years for a reverse mortgage to be cost-effective.

Number 6: Do I expect to receive any low-income assistance?

If you have relied on low-income assistance prior to retirement, it is likely you will continue to need assistance during retirement as health-care costs rise. Many seniors who have never received assistance before, especially widowed women, find themselves in need as they get older. Those receiving Supplemental Social Security Income, Medicaid, or other income-based assistance must talk with a government benefits specialist before taking out a reverse mortgage. The timing and amount of reverse mortgage payments needs to conform to the terms of the assistance plan so you will not risk losing the benefits.

Number 7: Do I have a well-balanced retirement plan and a clear reason for getting a reverse mortgage?

Reverse mortgages should not be used without careful thought. Just wanting some extra cash today is not a good reason for using a reverse mortgage. A reverse mortgage needs to work with, not against, your retirement expectations and personal and financial goals. Come up with a detailed budget and retirement plan and seek lots of advice.

Number 8: Do I understand how a reverse mortgage works and how it will fit into my personal plans?

By now you should have a good understanding of how a reverse mortgage works. Do not be hard on yourself, however, if you are still scratching your head; these are not simple or typical loans in any sense. Spend more time to understand how they work, and talk to a counselor or lender. Reverse mortgage products are constantly evolving, so talking to someone in the industry is the best way to get the latest information.

Number 9: Have I considered my alternatives?

Some financial planners say a reverse mortgage should be a last resort; this is probably an overstatement and an outdated view of the reverse mortgage market. But few would argue against seriously considering all of your options before getting a reverse mortgage. Think critically about your specific circumstances; you may have more options than you realize. Chapter 7 provides a good starting place for thinking about alternatives.

Number 10: Am I willing to reduce the inheritance that may one day go to my children?

Two conflicting values can come into play between reverse mortgages and inheritance; one is a desire to not be a burden to our children while we are living, and the other is a wish to leave them an inheritance when we are gone. If you need to use a reverse mortgage to retire independently and really want to leave money as a legacy, you will need to structure the reverse mortgage in a way that gives you what you need to live and also preserves as much equity as possible. Talk to your family members about using a reverse mortgage; they will most likely appreciate being included in your planning.

Conclusion

In case you missed the underlying message of this chapter, it derives from a Chinese proverb that goes like this: Someone who asks a question is only a fool for five minutes; someone who never asks a question is a fool forever. Answering the multitude of questions in this book, and, we hope, some of your own, should help you decide what a reverse mortgage is worth to you. If it is worth enough to proceed with one, then move on to the next section, where we discuss how to make it happen.

Part IV | Making It Happen

CHAPTER 9
The Reverse Mortgage Team

Choosing a reverse mortgage is a major life decision. Although reading books and surfing the Internet for information are great ways to learn about reverse mortgages, people will be your greatest asset in the reverse mortgage process. Taking out a reverse mortgage can raise difficult financial and emotional issues. Do not be afraid to ask for input from a variety of people. You never know whose wisdom will guide you to the best decision.

The Reverse Mortgage Team

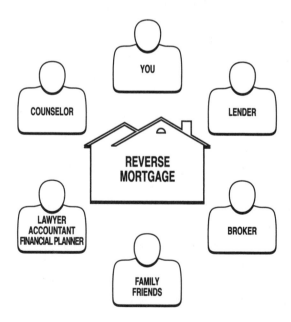

Choosing a Counselor

> *A word to the wise ain't necessary. It's the stupid ones who need the advice.*
>
> —Bill Cosby

Even the wise, or those who assume they are wise, will receive advice about reverse mortgages. As previously mentioned, every potential borrower is required to talk with a counselor before the reverse mortgage application is processed. Counselors provide unbiased information, and the session is free (at least it is with HUD-approved counselors), so there is no reason to object to this process. At a minimum, as required by law for HECMs, the session will cover the following:

- Alternatives to a reverse mortgage
- Home equity conversion options other than HECMs
- Financial implications of a HECM
- That HECMs may have tax consequences, affect eligibility for federal and state programs, and impact your estate
- Whether the homeowner has signed a contract with an individual or firm requiring payment of a fee for information about or access to HECMs or upon closing of a HECM

These points will be listed on the counseling certificate so that you can make sure they were discussed during the session.

The last point protects you from individuals and firms that charge fees in excess of legal amounts for information that you can access free from other resources. HUD has made sure that access to lenders, counselors, and other information about HECMs is free; you should never pay someone a fee to find a HECM lender for you. To the chagrin of estate-planning lawyers, sometimes these people advertise themselves as "estate planning" services.

Face-to-face counseling is preferred, but telephone counseling is acceptable in certain cases where face-to-face counseling is impracticable. Meeting in person would not be practicable if there is not a HUD-approved counseling agency within fifty miles of the borrower's home, or the local counseling agency does not provide counseling in the borrower's language. In cases in which the borrower is not legally competent, a person with a durable power of attorney or a court-appointed guardian or conservator may attend the session on the borrower's behalf.

It usually makes sense to start with a HUD-approved HECM counselor, because that person will also discuss the Home Keeper and other alternatives. Due to increasing demand for HECMs and the inability of borrowers to receive counseling in a timely manner, HUD approved an expanded network of HECM counselors in November 2005. That agency also agreed to continue to expand the network by administering a HUD-approved HECM counseling exam on a continuous basis across the country. There are several ways to locate a counselor; lenders, HUD or FHA, and AARP are a few of the places where you can obtain lists of approved counselors. A list of Web sites and phone numbers follows in this section.

If you have chosen a lender, it can provide you with a list of counselors. Lenders used to be required to provide a list of all approved counselors in the borrower's state. Since new regulations were passed in 2005, lenders are allowed to limit the list to five counselors. Lenders cannot contact a counselor for you, so do not be frustrated if they simply hand you a list. When it comes to counselors and lenders, never the two shall meet. Lenders are prohibited from recommending a particular counselor, and counselors are prohibited from recommending a particular lender.

If you do not have a lender yet, the simplest way to locate a list of approved HECM counselors is by clicking on your state on HUD's Web site at *www.hud.gov/offices/hsg/sfh/hecm/hecmlist .cfm* or by calling (800) 569-4287. As part of its goal to make sure there is enough good-quality counseling available, FHA has approved counselors from the agencies in the following list to be part of a National HECM Counseling Network, which provides face-to-face and telephone counseling across the country:

- National Foundation for Credit Counseling: *www.nfcc.org* or (800) 388-2227
- Money Management International: *www.moneymanagement .org* or (866) 889-9347
- AARP Foundation's Reverse Mortgage Education Project HECM Resources: *www.hecmresources.org/requests.cfm* or (800) 209-8085

Each of these agencies follows HUD's and FHA's counseling guidelines and has its own tests and requirements for counselors. For example, AARP Foundation Network counselors must pass a test administered by the AARP Reverse Mortgage Project. The counselors in this network meet regularly to compare stories, share information, and stay up to date.

Counselors use software to manipulate different loan types and payout options based on your financial input. The counselor will generate a printout for each option showing what you can expect to receive and to pay in costs. A big benefit of face-to-face counseling is that as you brainstorm and ask about different options, the counselor can generate new printouts for your immediate review.

It is important to be open and honest about your personal and financial information to get the most out of the counselor's analysis. Prepare for the session by first making sure you are eligible, and then gathering the following information:

- List of monthly and annual expenses and outstanding debts
- List of financial needs
- Explanation for why you want a reverse mortgage
- Approximate home value and condition of your home
- How long you expect to stay in your home

Counselors encourage you to bring family members, friends, or advisers with you to the session. If you do not mind openly discussing your finances, it may make sense to have someone else attend the session with you. Another person can provide moral support, objectivity, and serve as an extra set of eyes to check facts and details. Bringing family members to the session can clear up their concerns about inheritance and keeping the family home. Depending on your family, including them in the session may alleviate concerns or create tension. If you think family tension will frustrate the session, it may be best to attend by yourself or with a friend, and then go over the materials with your family at home. Sometimes when it comes to difficult family members, the less said, the better.

Make sure that you sign and obtain a certificate of counseling after the session is complete. You will not be eligible for a HECM or Home Keeper without proof of counseling. However, do not mistake the counseling certificate for instant loan qualification or take it as a sign that a reverse mortgage is right for you. Counselors are there to help you understand the issues, but ultimately, it is your choice.

Choosing a Lender

Once you decide a reverse mortgage is right for you, you need to find someone to originate the loan. This person will help you choose the best rate and loan for you and walk you through all of the paperwork for the loan. Most lenders are also loan originators. In this book, for simplicity, we use the terms "lender" and "originator" interchangeably. Technically, the lender is the one whose money you are borrowing, and the originator is the one who initiates the loan.

If you do not have a good referral from a friend or professional adviser, you should talk to several lenders and compare programs and costs. Luckily, there are many good resources for locating lenders. Borrowers who choose the HECM product can find a list of HECM lenders by state on HUD's Web site at *www.hud .gov*. Another good source is the National Reverse Mortgage

Lenders Association (NRMLA). Lenders who join the NRMLA must agree to abide by a code of conduct and be licensed in the state in which they are listed. A list of NRMLA members is found at *www.reversemortgage.org.*

While being a member of the NRMLA or any other organization is not a guarantee of ethical practices, it seems safest to choose a lender from this list. These lenders are more likely to be ethical, and they have access to the latest and best information about reverse mortgages. It also makes sense to use a lender that is licensed by your state, because the licensing requirements include such things as continuing education.

Of course, a lender may find you before you find it. If you are in the age range to qualify for a reverse mortgage, you may already be receiving mailings and advertisements from reverse mortgage lenders. Another way they reach out to potential borrowers is by speaking at community centers and public libraries. These seminars are free and may be a good way for you to gather current information about rates and options and to start asking questions of a lender.

Meeting with a lender can happen before or after the counseling session. It usually makes sense to meet with a counselor first so that you are well versed in reverse mortgages before you talk to the lender. Besides, the lender cannot go too far into the reverse mortgage application process with you until you provide proof of counseling. If you know a lender well and want to touch base with that person first, then do so for the sake of courtesy.

Here are some questions to help you prepare an agenda for talking with a lender:

- How long has the lender been offering reverse mortgages?
- Is it on the HUD list, or the NRMLA list, and is the lender licensed in your state?
- How much are its origination and servicing fees, and are they negotiable?
- Will the lender service the loan or sell it to another servicing company?

- If another company will service the loan, can the lender provide you with a sample account statement and explain it to you?
- Does the lender have the expertise you need; for example, HUD appraisals?
- Does it require background checks of its employees?
- Does it have materials that clearly explain the loan?
- Is the lender taking time to clearly explain the loan details to you and answer your questions?
- Can it provide loan analyses and comparisons that meet AARP's model specifications?
- Does the lender have a system for protecting your privacy and confidentiality?
- Is it interested in your particular circumstances?
- Are you comfortable with the lender, or do you feel pressured?

Remember, you are not obligated to originate the loan with someone just because he or she takes time to meet with you. If you are not comfortable or feel pressured, it may be best to shop around. If the lender is a reputable institution but you are not comfortable with the particular person who met with you initially, ask if you can meet with someone else within the organization.

Another party involved with your reverse mortgage on the lending side is the loan servicer or servicing lender. The originating lender and servicing lender may or may not be the same company. If they are different companies, the originating lender will provide you contact information for the servicing lender, but you will not meet with anyone there. The servicer is behind the scenes, using your monthly servicing fee to send you payments and statements, track your loan balance, and pay your property taxes and homeowners insurance.

Choosing a Mortgage Broker

Another way to originate a loan is to work with a mortgage broker. Mortgage brokers originate and process loans for several lenders. They too will advise you on loan options and walk you through all of the paperwork for the loan. Ultimately, however, the actual lender decides the rates and terms and whether to undertake the loan.

Mortgage brokers charge a fee for their services. Lenders do not pay or set these fees; broker fees are strictly between the customer and the broker. The fee may be financed in most cases, as long as the fee was permitted under applicable law and disclosed to the customer, and the broker actually performed advisory services and assisted with the loan application. The mortgage broker's fee will count as part of the total origination fee for HECMs.

Mortgage brokers must be licensed in the state in which they operate, so make sure anyone you work with is properly licensed. Mortgage brokers who are certified by the National Association of Mortgage Brokers (NAMB) must comply with the organization's code of ethics and best lending practices. NAMB members can be located through the NAMB home page at *www.namb.org.*

Seeking Advice

In addition to qualified reverse mortgage counselors, you may want to discuss a reverse mortgage with professionals, service providers, or other trusted advisers. They can provide insight beyond that of people within the reverse mortgage industry. Be aware that many professionals are just learning about reverse mortgages, so do not be surprised if they too have questions. Once they understand the basics, however, they will quickly be able to see the impact of a reverse mortgage on your personal, financial, and estate-planning goals.

Once you get immersed in researching reverse mortgages, it is easy to get lost in the details. Talking about a reverse mortgage with professional advisers can highlight connections, timelines, and alternatives that you may miss by brainstorming yourself. In other words, advisers can help you think outside of the reverse mortgage box and help you answer questions such as:

- How does a reverse mortgage impact other areas of my life?
- Do I need to make changes elsewhere to realign my priorities?
- I am not concerned about paying bills today, but what about in five to ten years?
- What are my lifetime financial goals?

You may bring a professional with you to the counseling session. If you are already working with a family attorney, accountant, or financial planner, he or she knows your financial history and estate-planning goals and will be able to help you get the most out of the counseling session. Attending the session will also help this adviser prepare for any changes to your estate plan, taxes, or financial portfolio related to the reverse mortgage. If your adviser is not going to attend the counseling session, at least inform him or her that you are looking into a reverse mortgage.

If you are not already working with one of these professionals, now may be the time to engage one. Professionals can help you sort through your financial history and develop goals. Their advice is based on specialized knowledge and real-life experience through their other clients. Financial planners may have ideas about retirement catch-up strategies that could help you prolong or eliminate the need for a reverse mortgage.

If you have been seeing a social worker or family counselor, especially if it is for family conflicts, you should talk to this person about how a reverse mortgage will impact your family. These advisers can help you with a plan for presenting the reverse mortgage to your family, and they will help you manage the stress of the reverse mortgage process. A reverse mortgage can be a major life change.

There are many not-for-profit advisers that you can speak with as well. For example, the local Area Agency on Aging (AAA) provides retirement planning education on a variety of topics. Before taking out a reverse mortgage due to financial need, you should talk with an AAA counselor to learn whether there are other options for covering day-to-day expenses, such as meals and transportation. The agency may be able to find a program or service to cover those costs so that home equity can be reserved for later, unexpected expenses.

Last on the list of potential advisers, but certainly not least, are your family and friends. These people have seen you through many other difficult decisions, and they will be there for you this time as well. Do not underestimate the power of the "friend of a friend" scenario. When discussing a reverse mortgage with one of your friends, that person may know someone who has used a reverse mortgage or, better yet, someone who is a reverse mortgage lender.

Knowing Your Rights

Most likely, all of the counselors, lenders, professionals, and advisers with whom you work will be honest and helpful. Plus, reverse mortgages are under the watchful eye of HUD and consumer groups, and are subject to many protective regulations. There will, however, always be some individuals who will try to take advantage of borrowers. Knowing your rights can help you avoid these individuals. You have the right to:

- Not close the loan even though you signed the loan application
- Receive a good faith estimate of the total loan costs
- Receive an itemized list of loan information
- Be told of any business arrangement between providers making referrals
- Cancel the loan within three days of closing

One of the most important rights to be aware of is that you are not obligated to complete a reverse mortgage transaction simply because you signed a loan application or received disclosures about reverse mortgage costs and terms. Federal Deposit Insurance Corporation (FDIC) Truth in Lending regulations require that consumers receive notice of this right as well as a good faith projection of the total annual loan cost, an explanation of the table of total annual loan cost rates, and an itemized list of pertinent loan information.

Truth in Lending regulations also entitle borrowers to a three-day right of rescission, or right to cancel the loan. Rescission is the undoing of a contract from the beginning (as if it never happened) and is different from termination, which can trigger repayment or other contract obligations. Lenders are required to provide a detailed notice of the right to rescind, including a form for that purpose. Borrowers may cancel the loan for any reason for up to three business days after the loan is closed or the lender delivers notice of the right to rescind, whichever is later.

Another regulation aimed at helping consumers make good borrowing decisions is the Real Estate Settlement Procedures Act (RESPA). Under RESPA, you have the right to certain disclosures when you apply for a loan, including a good faith estimate of settlement or closing costs and disclosure of any business arrangement between providers making referrals to one another. RESPA also prohibits anyone from giving or receiving kickbacks or anything of value in exchange for referrals of settlement service business, and from charging fees for services not actually performed.

In addition to these legal protections, your own common sense will keep predatory brokers and lenders from taking advantage of you. Never sign documents containing blank spaces or requiring you to pay expensive fees before closing the loan. Always ask about fees or charges that are not clearly documented. And be wary of people who make you feel pressured. There are many good and knowledgeable people in the reverse mortgage industry, so work with them.

CHAPTER 10

Choosing the Right Loan and Other Decisions

> *I was in the drugstore trying to get a cold medica-*
> *tion . . . not easy. There's the entire wall of products*
> *you need. You stand there going, well this one is*
> *quick acting but this one is long lasting. . . which*
> *is more important, the present or the future?*
>
> —Jerry Seinfeld

Choosing the right reverse mortgage can be as complicated as choosing a cold medicine. The options are many, and you must consider both present financial needs and what you want in the future. You must also compare the various options and choose the one that best fits your circumstances. In this chapter, we evaluate and compare the HECM, Fannie Mae Home Keeper, and Financial Freedom Cash Account Advantage; specifically:

- The maximum loan amounts available from each type of reverse mortgage
- The different methods of withdrawing the loan proceeds
- The total cost of each reverse mortgage, including the interest rates

Available Loan Amount

Lenders analyze several factors to determine the available loan amount. The weight given to these factors varies by lender and by reverse mortgage product. In Chapters 3 through 5, we discussed the specific factors that apply to the different reverse mortgage products. In this section, we discuss common themes that result from looking at each factor independently.

How Much Can I Get?

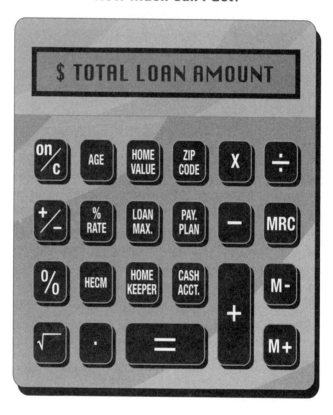

- **Age:** Older borrowers mean shorter-term loans and higher loan amounts.
- **Home Value:** Higher-value homes mean higher loan amounts.
- **Interest Rate:** Higher interest rates mean lower loan amounts.
- **Lending Limits:** Higher lending limits mean higher loan amounts. In most cases, rural areas have lower limits than do metropolitan areas.
- **Type of Reverse Mortgage Product:** HECMs typically have higher available loan amounts than other reverse mortgage products, unless the home is well above the national median home price, in which case a proprietary product may result in a higher loan amount. According to the National Association of REALTORS®, the national median existing home price in June 2006 was $231,000.

The sample worksheets on the following pages illustrate how available loan amounts vary among the HECM, Home Keeper, and Cash Account Advantage reverse mortgages. The loan amounts in the samples are based on estimated costs, interest rates, and loan limits as of November 2006. Monthly payment amounts are based on a tenure payment plan. These estimates assume there is no existing mortgage or other lien on the property that would need to be paid off and deducted from the total loan amount. Actual available loan amounts will vary depending on many factors, including the lender's underwriting practices, the current terms for each type of reverse mortgage, and interest rates.

Sample 1: 72-Year-Old Borrower in Scottsdale, Arizona, with a $250,000 House

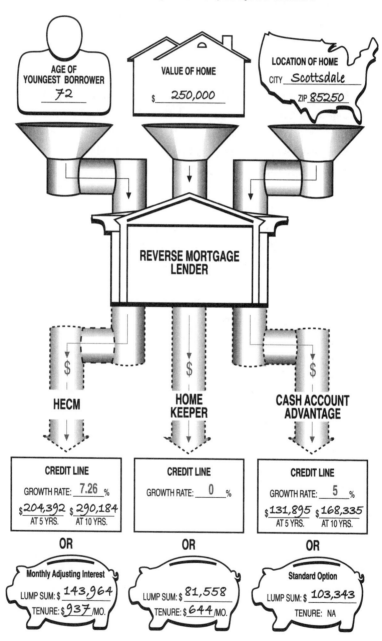

Sample 2: 72-Year-Old Borrower in Colorado Springs, Colorado, with a $350,000 House

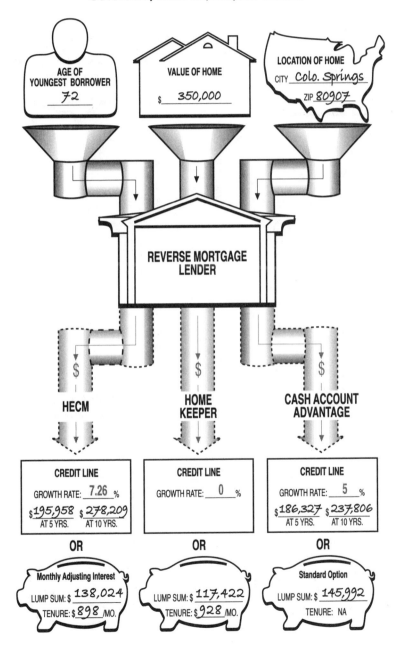

Sample 3: 72-Year-Old Borrower in Santa Barbara, California, with a $650,000 House

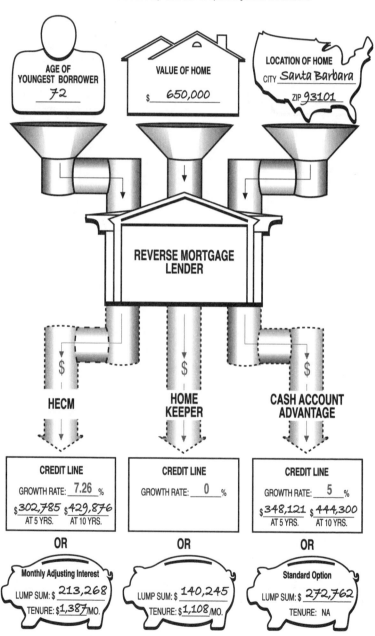

AGE OF YOUNGEST BORROWER
72

VALUE OF HOME
$ 650,000

LOCATION OF HOME
CITY Santa Barbara
ZIP 93101

REVERSE MORTGAGE LENDER

HECM

HOME KEEPER

CASH ACCOUNT ADVANTAGE

CREDIT LINE
GROWTH RATE: 7.26 %
$302,785 $429,876
AT 5 YRS. AT 10 YRS.

CREDIT LINE
GROWTH RATE: 0 %

CREDIT LINE
GROWTH RATE: 5 %
$348,121 $444,300
AT 5 YRS. AT 10 YRS.

OR

OR

OR

Monthly Adjusting Interest
LUMP SUM: $ 213,268
TENURE: $1,387/MO.

LUMP SUM: $ 140,245
TENURE: $1,108/MO.

Standard Option
LUMP SUM: $ 272,762
TENURE: NA

These samples are based on the youngest borrower being 72 years old. Age, however, can make a significant difference in the available loan amount. To illustrate the difference, following is a comparison of what the Scottsdale borrower with a $250,000 house would receive at various ages.

Age Makes a Difference

	HECM	Home Keeper	Cash Account Advantage Plan
62 years old	$119,047	$32,657	$74,843
72 years old	$143,964	$81,558	$103,343
82 years old	$171,521	$122,808	$122,543

We have included additional comparison worksheets in Appendix A. Try finding a sample that resembles your situation to get an idea of which program gives you the greatest loan amount at the right age. Appendix A also contains a fill-in-the-blank comparison worksheet for you to personalize with your own information. Visit one or more of the Web sites listed in Appendix C and use an online reverse mortgage calculator to complete your personalized comparison.

Once you know how much you could get, you need to consider how much you should take.

How Much Money Should You Take?

For many people, a reverse mortgage provides an opportunity to enjoy a better quality of life in their retirement years. Imagine having extra income every month for the rest of your life or having the security of an open line of credit with no repayment schedule. You might even use a portion of the proceeds to take a long-awaited vacation that you never felt you had the money or time for before.

Some experts in the reverse mortgage industry, however, feel that borrowers should not use reverse mortgage proceeds for just anything. "Home equity is a rainy day, last-resort kind of thing. It shouldn't be used to . . . go on vacation," says Ron Chicaferro, president of Thornburg Mortgage Home Loans Inc. in Santa Fe, New Mexico. Accordingly, most reverse mortgage borrowers today use their loan proceeds in a needs-driven way. AARP, in conjunction with HUD and FHA, surveyed reverse mortgage borrowers about how they use their reverse mortgage proceeds. These are the results:

Uses of Reverse Mortgage Proceeds

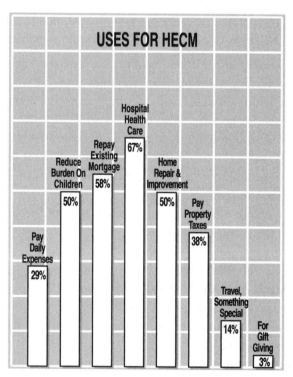

In Chapter 8 you learned that regardless of whether you save your equity for a rainy day or use the proceeds for a vacation, a reverse mortgage should be part of an overall financial and retirement plan, with careful consideration of the way the proceeds are withdrawn.

Avoiding the Poor Widow Scenario

Reverse mortgages require especially careful financial analysis for couples. If a couple takes out a reverse mortgage and spends most of the equity as a couple, the spouse who survives the other could be exposed to a greater risk of impoverishment. The survivor may also become home-locked, or unable to sell the home and relocate near family members due to the low amount of remaining equity in the home.

To make matters more difficult, studies show that a middle-class woman can quickly end up at poverty level after spending most of the couple's savings on the husband's long-term care. Obviously, the same thing can happen to a husband if his wife is first to suffer health problems. Do not underestimate the dramatic financial impact of long-term care.

Reserving a reverse mortgage for use by a widowed spouse could be like having an insurance policy. If the couple must use a reverse mortgage to meet their current financial needs, it is probably best to open a growing line of credit and withdraw only as much as necessary to meet those needs. That way, if one spouse dies, a sufficient line of credit will be waiting for the surviving spouse.

How Should You Receive the Money?

In addition to deciding how much money you should take from a reverse mortgage, you need to decide the form of payment. Does receiving a lump sum of cash or equal monthly payments better suit your needs? The payment options with each reverse mortgage program vary, so be sure to refer to the product-specific chapters (3 through 5) for more details. Following is a brief review of each payment option and the circumstances that tend to work best with that option.

Lump Sum Payment

The lump sum option is just as it sounds; the borrower receives the entire loan amount in one large payment after closing. All of the reverse mortgages discussed in this book allow the borrower to receive a lump sum. This option might work well if you need money to pay for a very large expense, such as a medical procedure. It may also be helpful if you want to eliminate a monthly mortgage payment by paying off your existing mortgage.

If you don't have a large and necessary expense, a lump sum is risky because it taps out all of your equity at once and the loan balance starts accruing interest right away. If you take a lump sum, you will have to be strict with yourself about spending the money wisely. You will also need a backup plan in case you need more money.

If you are not going to use the money right away, it may as well wait for you in a growing line of credit. It is unlikely you will find a conservative investment for the lump sum that will outperform the growing line-of-credit option. This is not the time in your life to speculate on risky investments with what may be your largest asset: your home equity.

Tenure Monthly Payment

Only the HECM and Home Keeper offer you the option of receiving a monthly payment for however long you have the loan. A lot of people like the sense of security that comes with a steady income. The monthly payment option can be good for those who need a little extra to cover daily living expenses on a regular basis and plan to remain in their home for many years.

There are a few drawbacks to the monthly payment option. Obviously, a low monthly payment will not help if you have a big unexpected expense. To prepare for the unexpected, you would need to save some of each monthly payment. In addition, the payments do not keep up with inflation. An extra hundred dollars per month might seem like a lot right now, but will it cover your living expenses in twenty years?

Term Monthly Payments

This monthly payment plan is similar to the tenure option, except that the payments will stop at the end of a fixed period. The borrower decides the fixed term; for example, five years. This option provides higher monthly disbursements than the tenure payment plan because the term of the loan will be shorter. However, when the term ends the payments will stop, so you will need to plan ahead to cover expenses at the end of the term. You will not have to repay the loan until you leave your home, but you will have tapped out all of your available equity at the end of the term.

The term payment option may work well for borrowers in need of extra monthly income for only a while. An example might be that you plan to sell your home in five years and move into an assisted living facility, but need help with monthly living expenses while you are still at home. If you choose a term plan, you really need to be as certain as possible about how long you will need the payments.

Line of Credit

While all of the reverse mortgage products discussed in this book provide a line-of-credit payment option, only the HECM and Financial Freedom lines of credit grow. Borrowers with a line of credit can withdraw amounts as they need money for extraordinary expenses, large purchases, or expenses that exceed the budget in certain months. It can also provide peace of mind by just being available for future expenses.

The best part is that the remaining available amount will grow at a reasonable interest rate (faster than most conventional savings accounts). This also provides some insulation from inflation. No wonder this is one of the most popular payment options.

While a line of credit is not as easy to squander as a lump sum, making withdrawals is not very difficult. So, if you are using this option, you should have a budget and financial plan to make disciplined use of the line of credit.

Combination Plan

The combination option allows you to tailor a payment plan to your circumstances by combining payment options. You can receive some cash up-front (as a lump sum or line of credit) and designate the rest to a monthly payment. This works well if you need a little extra help with monthly expenses but also want a reserve for emergencies.

Remember that most reverse mortgage products allow borrowers to change payment plans for a nominal fee. If, after closing, your circumstances change or you feel you made a mistake in selecting a payment plan, do not panic. Simply contact your lender and ask to make a change.

Comparison of Reverse Mortgage Costs

Many potential borrowers find that the costs of reverse mortgages outweigh the benefits, especially if they look into reverse mortgages as they approach age 62. Most people are aware that the high costs of reverse mortgages discourage a large number of people who can benefit from a reverse mortgage. However, it is likely that lenders and legislators will soon find a way to lower costs. Until that happens, there are a couple of things you can do to make sure the costs are justified.

First, do not rush to get a reverse mortgage as soon as you turn 62. The older you are, the higher your net loan amount will be, which makes the costs more justifiable. Paying a lot to get a little never makes sense. The best age to use a reverse mortgage right now seems to be between 72 and 75 years.

Second, stay in your home long enough to spread the costs. Paying a lot for a short-term benefit does not make sense either.

Most people agree that you should only get a reverse mortgage if you plan to stay in your home for at least five to seven years. Of course, these two points are made under ideal circumstances, and some people may need to use a reverse mortgage under circumstances that are less than ideal. In any case, borrowers should compare the costs of the different types of reverse mortgages to see which makes the most sense financially.

The Itemized Approach

An itemized approach to comparing costs is done by making a side-by-side comparison of the separate costs for each type of reverse mortgage. The detailed costs that apply to the HECM, Home Keeper, and Cash Account Advantage are discussed in Chapters 3, 4, and 5. Following is a review of the non-interest fees and costs applicable to most reverse mortgages that you may see in an itemized comparison.

- Origination fee
- Mortgage insurance premium (HECM only)
- Closing costs
- Servicing fees

Another itemized comparison that you may see is interest rates. If the loan is kept for an extended period of time, the interest paid on the principal will ultimately be the biggest cost. Therefore, you should compare the interest rates for each product. Before you can make a comparison, though, you need to understand how the rates are calculated.

All of the reverse mortgages discussed in this book have adjustable interest rates; that is, the interest rate changes periodically based on the change in an established interest rate index. The interest rate charged on the reverse mortgage is equal to the index base rate plus a margin established by the lender. Each of the reverse mortgage products has either a limitation on the extent of the adjustments during a set period of time and/or an absolute cap on interest rates. The following table shows the index base rate, margin, periodic rate adjustment, and caps for each reverse mortgage loan program.

Reverse Mortgage Interest Rates

	HECM		Home Keeper	Cash Account Advantage Plan
Index Base Rate	1-year Treasury Security (T-Bill)		1-month Certificate of Deposit	6-month London Interbank
Margin	3.1% for Annually Adjustable Rate Option OR	1.5% for Monthly Adjustable Rate	3.4%	3.5%
Periodic Rate Adjustments	Annual adjustment based on current T-Bill Rate plus Margin	Monthly adjustment based on current T-Bill Rate plus Margin	Monthly	Once every six months
Interest Rate Cap	Initial fully indexed rate + 2% annually with a maximum of + 5%	Initial fully indexed rate + 10%	Initial fully indexed rate + 12%	Initial fully indexed rate + 6%

As you can see, the interest rate for each type of loan depends on a different index base rate. The lender margins are set by law for the HECM and Home Keeper reverse mortgages. The periodic rate adjustments vary by product, and the borrower may have a choice of when the adjustment occurs; for example, biannually or annually. If the index base rates at time of closing were:

- 1-year Treasury Security (T-Bill): 5 percent
- 1-month Certificate of Deposit (CD): 5.25 percent
- 6-month London Interbank Offered Rate (LIBOR): 5.5 percent

Then each program would charge the following rates:

Sample Initial and Maximum Interest Rates

	HECM	Home Keeper	Cash Account Advantage Plan
Initial Fully Indexed Rate	8.1% annual adjustments 6.5% monthly adjustments	8.65%	9%
Maximum Fully Indexed Rate	13.1% annual adjustable 16.5% monthly adjustable	20.65%	15%

The initial fully indexed rate will be the actual interest rate charged at the beginning of the loan and equals the index base rate plus the lender's margin. The maximum fully indexed rate is the highest actual rate that could be charged on the loan. It is calculated by adding the index base rate plus the margin plus the maximum periodic rate adjustments. Fully indexed rates will most likely go up and down over the life of the loan, but will never exceed the maximum fully indexed rate allowed under the program's interest rate cap.

As you can see from the example, the HECM tends to offer the lowest interest rates. The loan balance will grow more slowly with a low interest rate. But this does not mean the HECM is always the lowest-cost option. Although comparing the itemized categories of each loan is straightforward, it is not that helpful for comparing the costs of one reverse mortgage to another. That is because different reverse mortgage products have different cost categories, and itemized costs do not reflect the true loan cost over the projected term of the loan.

Total Annual Loan Cost Comparison

The total annual loan cost (TALC) rate that is required to be provided to borrowers by Truth in Lending regulations is better than itemizing for comparing one reverse mortgage product to another. TALC is a single rate that includes all of the loan costs. It is intended to reflect the annual average cost of the loan expressed as an annual percentage of the projected total amount owed on the loan at a certain point in time. In addition to the TALC rate, the borrower will receive an explanation statement and an itemized list of the loan terms, charges, age of the youngest borrower, and the appraised property value.

The explanation statement will reveal that the cost of any reverse mortgage depends on two unknowns: (1) the loan period, which is based on how long you live, or live in your home, or whether there is a default that terminates the loan and (2) how your home value appreciates during that time. Because the TALC will vary based on these unknowns, the lender is required to provide TALC rates for three loan periods (two years, the borrower's life expectancy, and the borrower's life expectancy multiplied by a factor of 1.4) and three assumed annual appreciation rates (for example, 0 percent, 4 percent, and 8 percent).

The differences under these assumptions reveal that if you only plan to live in your home for a few years, the total cost of a reverse mortgage will be high, because the loan origination costs will still be a large part of the debt. TALC calculations show several important cost patterns:

- The annual average costs generally decrease over time.
- Reverse mortgages can be very expensive if they are repaid within the first few years.

- The costs can be moderate to low if the borrower lives in the home beyond her life expectancy and the home appreciates in value.
- TALC rates decrease over time as the loan balance rises and the costs become a smaller percentage of the loan balance.
- TALC rates can vary as much between the same loan types with different payment options as they do between different loan products.

The National Center for Home Equity Conversion provides a tutorial on how TALC rates are calculated on its Web site at *www.reverse.org/talctuto.htm.*

The TALC is an important consumer protection tool. Like all mathematical equations, however, it is based on assumptions that may prove wrong in a real-life scenario. First, the calculation is based on fixed interest rates, and most reverse mortgages come with adjustable rates. In a period of rising interest rates, the calculation may underestimate the true cost. Second, the regulations assume that borrowers who take out a credit line will draw 50 percent of the available amount at closing and not draw further advances during the term of the loan. The true cost of the loan will vary greatly depending on the size and timing of advances under a credit line arrangement. Third, the TALC is just one variable in the decision process; it does not take into account other financial information that a borrower may need to make decisions, such as how much leftover equity is desired.

Model Specifications

To address these limitations, the AARP Foundation's Reverse Mortgage Education Project (with a grant from HUD) developed a set of model specifications for a more customized approach to measuring reverse mortgage costs. In addition to calculating a total annual loan cost, these specifications provide rules for estimating the loan's total cash advances, total cost, and leftover equity. Determining the amount of leftover equity is important to borrowers who wish to leave some home value to their heirs.

The model specifications allow you to customize the figures by varying the loan period, home appreciation rate, and timing and size of cash advances. Borrowers using a line-of-credit payment option also need to select a withdrawal pattern based on the following options: a set amount per month, a set amount per year, or specific draws at specified times. Because the model specifications allow borrowers to input a specific withdrawal pattern for lines of credit, this method provides a more accurate estimate of total costs than does the TALC when borrowing with a line-of-credit payment option.

The model specifications have another advantage over the TALC rate: they show the effects of interest-rate fluctuations. One loan projection is based on the initial interest rate, and another is based on an expected interest rate. The AARP Foundation will continue to update and refine the specifications based on market developments and educational needs. The most current version of the model specifications is available on the AARP Web site at *www.aarp.org/revmort.*

By now you should have a sense of the complexity involved in assessing the costs and benefits of reverse mortgages. The good news is that much progress has been made and is under way to provide calculations that help borrowers make informed decisions. Be mindful, however, that none of these calculations are perfect; any figures you receive are estimates based on assumptions that may change.

Custom Loan Analysis

Even after you feel you have identified the reverse mortgage product that is right for you, remember that each loan product can produce different results based on age, home value, and payment plan. You may want to take the worksheets in Appendix A to your reverse mortgage counseling session and write in the various costs and calculations computed by your counselor.

After reading about each of the reverse mortgage products and how costs for each product can be compared, you should have a good idea of how reverse mortgages compare to one another. You may even know which loan would be best for you. The chapters that follow discuss the next steps: applying for and closing a reverse mortgage.

CHAPTER 11

Demystifying the Approval Process

> *What the world really needs is more love and less paperwork.*
>
> —Pearl Bailey

Deciding on a reverse mortgage product that best suits your circumstances is a major step in the right direction, but it is not the end of the road. The next step is to actually apply for the reverse mortgage loan. Here we move from the possible to the practical. This chapter covers the mechanics of how to get through the loan approval process for reverse mortgages. It includes everything from gathering information for the application to reviewing the loan closing documents; in other words, the paperwork.

Gathering Information

Gathering documents and information before meeting with a lender gives you credibility and makes the process run smoother for everyone. To that end, following is a list of personal and property information that you should gather and take with you when you meet with the lender.

Required Personal and Property Information

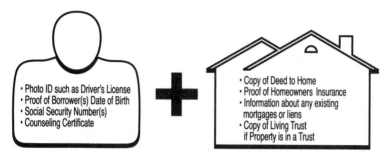

• Photo ID such as Driver's License
• Proof of Borrower(s) Date of Birth
• Social Security Number(s)
• Counseling Certificate

• Copy of Deed to Home
• Proof of Homeowners Insurance
• Information about any existing
  mortgages or liens
• Copy of Living Trust
  if Property is in a Trust

Most lenders consider the following documents acceptable proof of a borrower's date of birth and residency:

- Birth certificate
- Driver's license
- Passport
- Military ID
- Certificate of naturalization

State laws sometimes limit the types of identification that lenders can accept as valid proof of someone's age and residency. So, if a lender refuses a particular form of identification, it may just be complying with state law. If you do not have one of these documents, you should ask early in the process about acceptable alternatives.

Preparing the Application

To start the ball rolling after meeting with a counselor or lender, you will fill out a reverse mortgage loan application. For HECMs and Home Keepers, lenders may use the Residential Loan Application for Reverse Mortgages (Fannie Mae Form 1009) or the Uniform Residential Loan Application (Fannie Mae Form 1003). A HUD/VA Addendum is also required for HECMs. Some key sections of a typical application are discussed in the next sections to familiarize you with this document.

Number 1: Payment Plan

The borrower is required to select a payment plan, whether fixed monthly payments, lump sum payment, line of credit, or a combination. Do not worry about being locked into a plan; this selection is meant to indicate your interest to the lender. You are free to change the payment plan prior to closing.

Number 2: Property Details

Since reverse mortgage eligibility is tied to a principal residence, the borrower's primary residence should be entered in the property address section. There is a check-the-box section for residence type; in almost all cases, "primary residence" should be checked. However, if you reside in a multi-unit property with rental tenants, then you will need to check both "primary residence" and "investment property." A legal description is also requested, which can typically be pulled from the title commitment or existing policy or survey and attached if it is too long for the space provided. The legal description can also be found on the deed to the property.

Number 3: Estimate of Appraised Value

The application asks for an estimate of the property value. At this stage, all you can do is use your best guess. Perhaps you have heard what a similar home in your neighborhood sold for recently, or you can look at home sales listings in your local newspaper. There are a number of online tools to help you get an idea of the market value of your house. One popular Web site is *www .zillow.com;* it provides a free estimate of your home value based on recent sales in your area. A formal appraisal will be scheduled later in the process, so the lender does not expect an exact valuation on the application.

Number 4: Property Title

This form requires you to list all legal titleholders to the property and how they hold title. Property title may be held as a fee simple, life estate, or leasehold estate. If you are not sure about the exact wording of the titleholders' names, you can find them on the deed to your property. You may have the original deed in your files, and a copy is normally available at the county land recorder's office. Many counties now post this information free on the Internet.

Number 5: Monthly Income and Assets

The application asks you to identify monthly income and a list of available assets, even though the loan is not based on your income or assets other than your home. This is probably because the same forms are used for home purchase or forward mortgages. So, do not worry; your income or lack thereof will not be a barrier to qualifying for a reverse mortgage.

Number 6: Liens

You will need to list all outstanding liens or debts against the property. For example, list any amounts you still owe on a purchase mortgage, or government liens from failure to pay property taxes or other assessments. If you recently paid off a judgment or lien, bring proof with you in case the county records are not up to date. You may want to run a credit report before meeting with the lender if you have a history of credit problems. Remember, the reverse mortgage lender will want to be in a first lien position, so any existing mortgages or liens on your home will need to be paid off either separately or with the reverse mortgage proceeds.

Number 7: Signature

It goes without saying that you must sign the loan application. By signing, you certify that the information you provided in the application is true and correct and acknowledge that you can face civil and criminal penalties for intentional or negligent misrepresentations. Never lie on a loan application. Signing the application does not, however, commit you to taking out a loan. You can still change your mind.

Reviewing the Numbers

After the application is complete, and as required by Regulation Z, the lender will provide you with a good faith estimate of the total annual loan cost (TALC), which reduces all of the costs and fees associated with the loan to a single projected rate. This can help you decide whether the proceeds from a reverse mortgage outweigh the costs based on the lender's projection of the total loan costs. Remember, TALC is based on assumptions including the home's projected appreciation and the term of the loan. The lender will also provide a reverse mortgage comparison for each product and payment option, including the total loan amount for each option.

You may have already reviewed a lot of printouts and numbers with the counselor or by yourself using online calculators. The good faith estimate and comparison that you receive at this point is the closest thing to the final loan numbers that you will have seen. It is specific to the lender, your circumstances, the reverse mortgage product, and current interest rates and other costs. That said, these numbers are not guarantees, and may change as interest rates and other circumstances fluctuate before and after closing. For example, the lender does not know how long you will have the loan, whether interest rates will go up or down, or how your home will appreciate, so these costs are only estimates.

Tax and Insurance Election

You will need to decide how to manage property taxes and hazard insurance premiums with a reverse mortgage. Staying current on these payments is very important to prevent a default under the loan agreement. Most lenders will not terminate the loan for one missed or late payment, but they have the right to do so. Since termination means you will have to pay off the loan, it is best to not take risks here.

A safe choice is to have the lender make these payments for you. The lending institution can arrange to pay taxes, insurance, or both. For mortgages with a monthly payment plan, the lender will reduce monthly scheduled payments by an amount equal to $\frac{1}{12}$ of the estimate of taxes and insurance for that year and place the funds in a set-aside account until the payment dates. For mortgages with a line-of-credit payment plan, the lender will treat the payment of taxes and insurance as an unscheduled payment. However, once the principal limit has been reached and no more disbursements are available, the borrower is once again responsible for paying these items directly from his or her own funds.

While electing to have taxes and insurance withheld by the lender reduces the total principal loan amount available to you, it may be worth the peace of mind. Many people who have home purchase or forward mortgages choose to have the lender pay the taxes by collecting them with the regular monthly payments. Lenders are happy to do this because it protects their security interest, and borrowers are relieved of managing one more payment. A form will be provided during the application process for you to make this election.

Property Appraisal

Once the loan application is signed, the lender will begin processing the loan. To start, the lender will verify your personal information and request a credit report and title search. If the credit report turns up any state or federal tax liens or outstanding federal debt, these amounts must be paid off at or before closing. Next, it will order an appraisal and any required inspections.

The appraisal will determine your home's market value. It is based on how much comparable homes in your area are selling for, and the condition of your home. The appraisal is a critical step in the reverse mortgage process, because it is one of the factors the lender will use in determining the loan amount that is available to you.

The lender will contact an appraiser to set up an appointment with you. Appraisers are licensed professionals who must comply with strict ethical standards. Given the importance of the appraisal to your loan amount, it is best to cooperate with the appraiser. When working with an appraiser be flexible, available, prepared, and polite.

Be Flexible. Most appraisers have tight schedules, so try to be as flexible as possible when making an appointment. Also, keep in mind that they will need full access to your home and yard. Keep pets, especially dogs, secure and out of the way. Unlock interior and exterior gates and doors.

Be Available. While you are not required to be home during the appraisal, it is best to be there to answer questions and explain any unusual features of the home. If you absolutely cannot be home that day, schedule a time to talk with the appraiser on the telephone. It is in your best interest to answer questions; otherwise, the appraiser may assume the worst about a particular issue or condition with your home.

Be Prepared. There are several things you can do to prepare for the appraisal. Put together a file with home improvement records and dates of remodels, paint jobs, and appliance purchases. Most important, clean up the interior and exterior of the house and make any small repairs that you can afford. Remember, the lender will require necessary repairs to be made or loan funds set aside for the repairs. You may not even qualify for a reverse mortgage if your home requires too many repairs.

Be Polite. The appraiser will want some alone time to look around and evaluate your home. Answer questions, but do not distract him with long stories about the history of your home, and never offer more than is asked. The appraiser needs time to measure square footage, draw a floor plan, check the condition of the home and appliances, and take photographs.

The appraisal is one of the third-party costs that the borrower is responsible for paying. You may have to pay the appraiser at the time he or she visits your home. Sometimes the lender will collect the fee with the reverse mortgage application; at other times, the lender will cover the cost and be reimbursed at closing. Even if the loan does not close, you will have to pay the appraiser for the work.

The appraiser usually takes less than one week after a visit to complete the appraisal document and deliver it to the lender. The appraisal will state the home's value and identify conditions that need repair. If you disagree with the appraisal, it is best to talk to the lender about it and request a review. Ordering a second appraisal costs more than the review fee and usually does not accomplish anything, because the lender will use the lower of the two values.

Required Repairs

If the lender finds that repairs to the property are required as a condition to making the loan, a repair rider will be added to the loan agreement. Typical repairs include leaky roofs, bad wiring or plumbing, termite damage, and rickety staircases. Most lenders require that any necessary repairs be completed within twelve months of the loan closing date. If they are not completed by this deadline, the lender may stop making disbursements or advances.

There are two ways to manage repairs. One is to make the repairs before the loan closes. This is probably the best option for minor repairs. Another option is to set aside some of the loan funds in a repair escrow account. The lender will escrow an amount greater than the repair estimate to be safe, normally one and one-half times the estimated cost. The lender also may charge a small fee for administration of the repair fund.

The cost of the repairs may influence how they are managed. Estimated repairs of less than 15 percent of the maximum loan amount can usually be completed after closing. If the estimated repairs are greater than 15 percent of the loan amount, they may have to be completed before closing. Properties needing really major repairs, greater than 30 percent of the loan amount, may not be eligible for a reverse mortgage.

The lender will usually monitor the progress of the repairs and will not disburse funds from the repair set-aside until it receives a certificate of completion or other acceptable documentation (for example, a punch list) that the work has been completed as agreed. The borrower may request in writing that the funds be paid directly to the contractor. An appraiser will reinspect the home to check the repairs and will tell the lender whether the work is completely satisfactory.

What happens if the funds in the repair set-aside are lesser or greater than the actual cost of the repairs? If all of the funds in the repair set-aside were not needed, the unused portion will be added to the borrower's line of credit. On the other hand, if the funds in the repair set-aside were insufficient to cover the actual repair costs, additional funds will be taken from the borrower's line of credit.

Reviewing Closing Documents

Before the closing, the loan documents and final figures will be prepared. This is the time to dive into the details and make sure the documents and figures reflect your discussions with the lender and your understanding of how the reverse mortgage works. It can be costly and frustrating to make changes after the closing, so speak up now if something does not match your understanding. If the closing has to be rescheduled, the final figures will change to reflect interest rate fluctuations.

The final figures will include the cash being disbursed to you and the itemized closing costs, which are usually financed as part of the loan. The numbers are presented in a settlement statement and should be similar to the numbers in the good faith estimate you received at the start of the loan process. Take time to review the statement and ask about changes from the estimate.

The closing documents should also be available to review before the closing. These documents are too lengthy to review in detail at the actual closing. Plus, if you want an attorney to review the documents, he or she will need time to do so before closing. If you are working with an attorney, let the lender know so that it can get you the documents as soon as possible. The primary loan documents that will be signed at closing are a promissory note, a mortgage or deed of trust, and a loan agreement. There are many other documents you will sign at closing, but those are the primary loan documents. An overview of each of the main closing documents follows.

Promissory Note

A promissory note, as its name implies, contains your promise to repay the reverse mortgage debt. Due to the unique nature of reverse mortgages, you may notice a couple of strange provisions in the note. First, all promissory notes must have a maturity date or date on which the loan is to be repaid. Since reverse mortgages do not need to be repaid until the borrower leaves the home (an uncertain deadline), the maturity date is often set at fifty years after the youngest borrower's 100th birthday. Second, all promissory notes must state the principal loan amount. For reverse mortgages, this amount is uncertain because the borrower may or may not withdraw the entire available loan amount, so the amount shown on the promissory note will likely be a function of the maximum available loan amount.

Mortgage or Deed of Trust

The mortgage or deed of trust (depending on your state's laws) is a document that creates a lien against your home to secure repayment of debt and defines your obligations with respect to the secured property. It is what enables the lender to foreclose and sell the home if you or your heirs fail to repay the loan when it is due. In some states this document is referred to as a mortgage, and in others as a deed of trust. This document will be filed in the county property records so that anyone interested knows that the reverse mortgage lender has a priority security interest in the home.

Loan Agreement

The loan agreement sets forth the terms of the loan including all the rights and obligations of the lender and borrower with respect to the loan. The lender is required to give a copy of the loan agreement to you for review prior to closing, and is allowed to give you a copy of the loan agreement form before the counseling session. The counselor will go over the basic provisions with you, but he or she is not an attorney, and so will limit comments to key features of typical loan agreements.

Following is a look at several of the main sections found in most loan agreements.

Parties: The first paragraph of the loan agreement will contain blanks for the name of the borrower, any co-borrowers, and the lender. The HUD Secretary will also be a party to the HECM loan agreement.

Definitions: As in many other kinds of agreements, the first article of a loan agreement contains definitions of all of the terms used in the agreement. Many people glaze over the definition section, but it is the basis for the rest of the agreement and should be carefully reviewed. Refer back to the definition section every time you encounter a defined term in the agreement.

Loan Advances: One article or section of the loan agreement will be dedicated to describing the loan advances made to the borrower. This is usually the longest section of the loan agreement and is really the meat and potatoes of the agreement. It covers any initial advances for closing costs and discharging of prior liens. If property repairs are required, this section will describe how much will be set aside and how it will be applied. It covers all of the payment plan details, such as when advances are made, how they are applied to the loan limit and balance, and how interest and mortgage insurance premiums are calculated. This section also contains details about how to change payment plans.

Finally, it describes the lender's right to protect the property by withholding amounts for taxes and special assessments. The lender has the right to make reasonable expenditures to protect the property from condemnation and similar proceedings, and to add those expenses to the loan balance.

Late Charges: You do not need to make payments on the reverse mortgage, so the late charges section does not typically apply to borrowers. If a HECM lender fails to make a timely payment to the borrower, it will be charged a penalty fee by HUD. This late charge is paid by the lender from its own funds to the HUD Secretary.

Termination: The termination article describes the circumstances under which a lender may stop making loan advances to a borrower. For example, a lender may stop making advances if the borrower files bankruptcy or if the lender's lien status is jeopardized. The lender will also stop making advances if the borrower pays off the loan in full.

HUD Obligation: HECM loan agreements contain a provision describing HUD's obligation to make loan advances to the borrower if the lender defaults or can no longer make payments. Essentially, in such a case the loan agreement is assigned to HUD, and HUD steps into the shoes of the lender. HUD must notify the borrower of any changes to procedures for handling requests for payments or changes in payment plans resulting from the assignment.

Miscellaneous Section: Most agreements contain a miscellaneous section that covers matters that do not fit in other sections but are still important to the agreement. This section will name the law that will govern the agreement, typically the law of the state in which the property is located. It will identify where to send notices under the agreement, and how those notices should be sent.

Exhibits: The loan agreement will contain exhibits with borrower-specific financial information, such as the available loan amount, payment plan, and a schedule of closing costs.

Riders: If property repairs are required, the loan agreement will contain an attachment known as a repair rider that will set forth the repair obligations.

Underwriting and Approval

After all of the paperwork is complete, your reverse mortgage application package will go through a process called underwriting. Some lenders have in-house underwriters; others use a third party. The underwriter makes sure the loan documents are complete and, ultimately, approves or disapproves the loan. The underwriting process can take anywhere from a few weeks to a couple of months. Once the lender receives underwriting approval, it is time to schedule the closing and receive your funds. The next chapter covers the closing, and managing the reverse mortgage after closing.

Part V | Other Important Considerations

CHAPTER 12

Closing and Managing a Reverse Mortgage

The reverse mortgage application and underwriting process may take several weeks or maybe even several months, but it will culminate in a single event known as the closing. You probably remember the closing that occurred when you purchased your home with a forward mortgage. Reverse mortgage closings are similar, except you are not buying or selling your home. In this case the closing is the meeting at which the loan documents are signed and the mortgage begins. This chapter covers the closing as well as how to manage the reverse mortgage after the closing.

Closing

The lender will contact you to schedule a closing once the loan application is approved. Each borrower typically attends the closing. However, a borrower may sign the documents in advance if he or she is unable to attend the closing, or have someone else sign the documents for him or her by power of attorney. We discuss the specific requirements for using power of attorney in Chapter 13. Also attending will be the lender, a notary, and an agent from the title company.

Closings can take an hour or more to get through the paperwork and signatures, but they are fairly straightforward. You have already made the tough decisions about loan products and payment options. You also should have had time before closing to review most of the loan documents with your advisers and make any necessary changes or corrections.

Even though you have seen most of the information before the closing, the lender will review the type of loan and payment option that you chose and go over your obligations under the loan agreement. The lender will also calculate the actual closing costs and review the final settlement statement and total annual loan cost with you. Up to this point, all of the numbers have been estimates based on an expected interest rate.

This expected interest rate is usually pretty close to the actual rate that will determine your loan amount at closing, but it depends on the financial markets and how much time has passed between the initial application and the closing date. Because there is an inverse relationship between interest rates and loan amounts, your loan amount or principal limit may be higher or lower than expected.

If, however, you are using a HECM and were able to lock the expected interest rate at the time you signed the reverse mortgage application, the principal limit at closing will be identical to the amount in the good faith estimate (this is referred to as a principal limit lock). Since the lock is only good for sixty days, be sure to close within that time frame, especially if interest rates have been going up. Of course, you should choose a new rate in the event that interest rates decreased before closing, since that will enable you to receive more money than the original estimate.

Do not be afraid to ask questions about anything new or unfamiliar in the loan documents. Some changes can be made at the closing if there is an error in the paperwork, but others will require rescheduling the closing. It is better to reschedule the closing and postpone receiving your funds for a few days than to sign something with which you do not agree.

When the numbers and other documents have been reviewed and agreed upon, the borrower and any co-borrowers will sign all of the closing documents and loan papers required to finalize the loan. The primary documents of the loan transaction that will be signed at closing are:

- Promissory note
- Mortgage or deed of trust
- Loan agreement
- Settlement statement
- Disclosures about costs, fees, taxes, and insurance
- Repair addendum, if applicable

Signing can take a while, because three or more originals are required and several documents must be notarized. A notary is a person legally empowered by the state to witness signatures and certify a document's validity. Do not jump ahead and start signing; wait for the notary to witness your signature.

After the closing papers are signed, a title company will record the mortgage or deed of trust with the appropriate county office. The title to your home will remain in your name, but the reverse mortgage will be a lien on your property. The same thing happened when you bought your home with a forward mortgage. The lien secures the repayment of the loan by encumbering the property so that if the borrower or the heirs do not repay the loan, the lender can have it sold through the foreclosure process and get repaid.

Funding

You will not receive any money at closing. Remember the three-day right of rescission? Because you have the right to cancel the loan for up to three days after closing, the loan will not be funded until the rescission period passes. Otherwise, the lender would have to take back any funds that were disbursed if you changed your mind.

Canceling the loan at this point should be rare, since a lot of thought and counseling led up to deciding to apply for a reverse mortgage. If you do have any doubts, talk through them with your family or counselor. You should only cancel for a major reason, such as realizing you got a bad deal or learning that you will not be able to continue living in your home as long as expected. Of course, it is your legal right and prerogative to cancel for no reason.

Once the rescission period ends, you will be able to receive money from the reverse mortgage. How you receive the money depends on the payment option that you chose. If you chose a monthly payment option, the funds can be automatically deposited into your bank account. Direct deposits are safe and easy, but if you prefer, you can also receive a check each month and deposit it yourself. Lump sum payments are made by check, which you can pick it up or have mailed to you. To receive payments from a line of credit, you need to fill out a withdrawal request form and either mail or fax it to the lender. The withdrawal can be directly deposited in your bank account, or you can receive a check.

Now that the reverse mortgage is funded, you should be able to breathe easier. For those who needed the funds to make ends meet, be proud that you have done everything possible to meet your needs. For those seeking peace of mind, relax. And for those who wanted to treat themselves to something special, enjoy it. The difficult emotional and financial questions related to reverse mortgages are behind you.

Ongoing Obligations

Breathe a sigh of relief after the closing, but do not forget that, even though you do not need to make monthly payments to repay the loan, there are still ongoing obligations under the loan agreement. Most of these obligations are simply keeping up with matters that were necessary to qualify the property for a reverse mortgage in the first place. Other obligations are more administrative and relate to managing the loan itself. These ongoing obligations include:

- Paying insurance and taxes
- Certifying occupancy
- Maintaining the property
- Reviewing monthly statements

Insurance and Taxes

Borrowers are responsible for timely payment of homeowners insurance premiums as well as state and local property taxes. To be eligible for the reverse mortgage, you had to show adequate homeowners insurance. Because the home is the only security for the loan, the lender wants to be able to repair or replace the property if it is significantly damaged. You may have had to increase the amount of insurance coverage based on the appraisal so that the lender will be covered for the full amount of the loan.

Lending institutions are concerned about keeping taxes current, because a government tax lien is one of the few things that have precedence over a lender's mortgage lien. That means the government will get paid first if your home is sold, and the lender will have to be satisfied with whatever is left over. So, you can see why lenders reserve the right to stop payments and terminate the loan if you do not pay your tax bill on time.

Ideally, you were able to arrange for the lender to make property insurance and tax payments for you. That is the safest and easiest way to manage these matters. If you make payments yourself instead of having the lender do it for you, the lender may ask you to provide proof of payment before the penalty date. Be sure to keep all receipts and records of payment for these items in case the lender requests proof.

Certifying Occupancy

Remember that to be eligible for a reverse mortgage, your home must be your principal residence. If you do not keep using your home as a principal residence, the loan will become due and payable. There are a couple of reasons why occupancy is so important. First, the raison d'être of reverse mortgage programs is to provide the money necessary to enable people to remain in their homes. Second, since the lender is waiting to be repaid from the proceeds of the sale of the home and is taking significant risks in doing so, it is important that you live in and take care of the home.

To make sure that this is the case, once each year the lender will ask you to sign a document certifying that the property is your principal residence. The certification requests are usually sent within 30 days of the anniversary date of the first day of the first month after closing. You are usually given thirty days to sign and return the certification. You will probably also be asked to inform the lender in writing any time you spend more than two months away from home. To avoid a determination that the home is no longer a principal residence, you should promptly respond to all such requests and sign and return any certifications.

Maintaining the Property

Borrowers have an obligation to make required repairs and maintain the property. Recall from Chapter 11 that if the appraiser found the property in need of repairs, a repair rider will be part of the loan agreement. If the repairs are not completed by the lender's deadline, the lender may stop making disbursements or advances. A repair escrow account may have been set up to cover the cost of the repairs.

The lender will monitor the progress of the repairs and will not disburse funds from the repair set-aside until it receives acceptable documentation from the appraiser that the work has been completed as agreed. Any unused funds from the set-aside will be added to the borrower's line of credit. If the funds in the repair set-aside were insufficient to cover the actual repair costs, additional funds will be taken from the borrower's line of credit.

Even after necessary repairs have been made, you are required to maintain the property in a condition satisfactory to the lender. This condition is at least equal to the condition the home was in on the closing date. For HECMs, the property needs to meet

FHA's minimum property standards. It should not be too difficult to meet these standards as long as you regularly clean your home, perform seasonal maintenance, and make necessary repairs in a timely manner.

The servicing lender may make drive-by inspections of the property. If you do not keep the property in good condition and repair, the servicer may determine there is a default and call the loan due and payable. Most servicers will make every effort to work with a borrower in default of the maintenance provision. They will detail the repairs necessary to bring the property back into compliance and may even revise the loan payment plan so that a line of credit can be used to fund the repair costs. However, if the borrower does not cooperate to make necessary repairs, the servicer will request the loan be made due and payable.

If a sudden illness or disability prevents you from keeping your home in good condition and repair, seek help immediately. Ask a family member or neighbor for help. If that is not possible, your local Area Agency on Aging may be able to connect you with someone who can help with cleaning and maintaining your home at little or no charge.

Reviewing Monthly Statements

The lender or loan servicer usually has some obligation to send you regular statements with details about your reverse mortgage. Home Keeper statements are required to be sent at least on a quarterly basis. HECM statements are sent once each year, by January 31. The statements include the following information:

- All monthly payments and line-of-credit draws and balances
- All payments made on the borrower's behalf for servicing fees, taxes, and insurance
- All of the interest rate changes and the total interest accrued
- The loan balance as of the end of the statement period

Some state and local laws require that statements be sent more frequently and contain more detailed information about the interest rates and index values. You should review these statements and monitor the outstanding loan balance. The statements should be placed in a file and located with your other financial information.

Spending the Money Wisely

Now that you have closed the loan and are receiving payments or drawing on a line of credit, it is time to consider how best to spend the money. Withdrawing all of the available funds too early can leave you without any safety net. Once you reach the maximum available loan limit, you will not be able to withdraw any more funds. If you chose a tenure monthly payment plan, you are insulated from this mistake because you are guaranteed to receive the same monthly payment for as long as you live in your home.

The timing and amount of cash that you withdraw from a line of credit impacts the remaining amount of credit available, the total amount owed, and the total annual average cost of the loan. The AARP provides a calculator at *www.rmaarp.com* that computes the effect of various withdrawal patterns on a year-by-year basis. A growing line of credit is clearly the best option, since it will refurbish itself as you make withdrawals.

It goes without saying that reverse mortgage funds should not be invested in risky ventures. Home equity makes up the greater part of most people's wealth. It is an irreplaceable asset in the sense that it took years to pay down your forward mortgage and benefit from appreciation. You do not want to find that at age 85 you no longer have any savings or equity on which to rely.

Therefore, make a budget and stick to it; have a solid plan for how to spend your reverse mortgage funds. Always keep in mind your ongoing loan obligations when preparing a budget. You need to make sure you have enough money to maintain the property and pay taxes and insurance, since failure to do these things may make the loan due and payable. If your loan balance starts approaching your limit, meet with a financial planner or CPA to develop a plan for paying down the loan or preserving as much of the balance as possible.

Changing the Payment Plan

As you may recall from Chapters 3 to 5, for a nominal fee, borrowers may change their payment plan at any time and as many times as they choose. The most obvious change is to switch from one type of payment plan to another but other types of changes include:

- Suspending payments for a period of time
- Withdrawing an unscheduled amount
- Changing the amount of—or, for HECMs, the term—of monthly payments
- Reducing the amount of monthly payments and adding a line of credit

Before making any changes, run the proposed change through a reverse mortgage calculator to see how it impacts your loan.

Refinancing the Loan

As with any other mortgage, refinancing a reverse mortgage is possible. However, the relatively high cost of a reverse mortgage makes it unlikely that refinancing will make economic sense. The value of a home would have to dramatically increase, or interest rates would have to dramatically decrease, in order to justify the costs. As the reverse mortgage market grows and products evolve, the costs of reverse mortgages will likely go down, which may eventually result in refinancing becoming more practical.

Repaying the Loan

Even though reverse mortgages do not have a predetermined maturity date like forward mortgages, reverse mortgages are loans that must be repaid at some point as discussed in Chapters

3 to 5. When it is time to repay the reverse mortgage, the loan must be repaid in one final payment. This payment includes the sum of the loan disbursements or advances and accrued interest. Because reverse mortgages are non-recourse loans, the amount of the full repayment will never be more than the market value of the property. If the loan balance is greater than the home's value, the lender will have to accept the market value of the home as repayment in full.

In most cases, the loan is paid off with the proceeds from the sale of the borrower's home. Most lenders will give you or your heirs a reasonable period of time to sell the home. If you are not able to sell the home, the lender will initiate foreclosure proceedings and add the cost of those proceedings to the outstanding loan balance. If you or your heirs have other assets, those assets may be used to pay off the loan so that the house can remain in the family.

Of course, you may voluntarily repay the entire loan balance or part of it. You may want to make a partial prepayment to preserve more equity or to increase the amount of your monthly payments or available line of credit. Paying off the loan in full will probably terminate the loan, so consider whether you want to keep a small balance to maintain the loan. Otherwise, if the loan terminates, you will be back at square one and will need to reapply for a reverse mortgage if you want to convert any more of your equity into cash. Imagine going through this process twice!

CHAPTER 13

Special Circumstances and Considerations

No two homeowners are alike, and no two homes are alike. Therefore, it is possible that you have special circumstances that will affect how your home is treated for the purposes of a reverse mortgage. This chapter covers unique real estate matters and certain technical aspects of estate planning that impact reverse mortgages.

Real Estate

Throughout the book we talk about how the HECM eligibility requirements for property include meeting FHA property guidelines. In essence, FHA property guidelines require that the property be safe, sanitary, and in good repair. The guidelines cover all aspects of the exterior, interior, and site condition of the home as well as unique requirements for each type of property. A property appraisal is done to determine whether the condition of the property meets guidelines and is acceptable for FHA mortgage insurance purposes.

The appraisal and property guidelines are found in the first chapter of the HUD-FHA Single Family Housing Homeownership Center Reference Guide. The guidelines are much too lengthy to reproduce here, but you can find them on HUD's

Web site at *http://www.hud.gov/offices/hsg/sfh/ref/chap1.cfm.* HUD-approved reverse mortgage counselors can help answer questions about whether your property qualifies for a HECM or Home Keeper reverse mortgage.

In this chapter we discuss some of the most common real estate circumstances related to:

- Condominiums
- Excess land
- Manufactured and modular homes
- Private roads and shared driveways
- Leasehold interests
- Homestead advisory
- Wells and septic systems
- Wood stoves and space heaters

Condominiums

The word *condominium* is actually a legal term used to define a type of joint ownership of real property in which portions of the property are commonly owned and other portions are individually owned. Normally, a condominium owner has exclusive ownership of the unit and joint ownership in the common areas (for example, hallways and recreational facilities). A homeowners association manages the common areas through a board of directors elected by the owners of the units.

It was not until 1961 that FHA was allowed to insure mortgages on condominiums. This change dramatically increased the number of condominiums sold in the United States and, therefore, the number of condominium owners. Because so many people own condominiums, it is important to know what is necessary for a condominium to be eligible for a reverse mortgage.

To be eligible for a HECM reverse mortgage, the condominium must be located in a condominium project that has FHA approval. If the condominium project in which you live is not FHA approved, it is still possible to be approved for a HECM through HUD's "spot approval" loan program. To be eligible, the condominium project must:

1. Have been managed by the association for at least one year
2. Not have any restrictions on conveyance, such as a right of first refusal
3. Have sold 90 percent of the units
4. Be at least 51 percent owner-occupied; in other words, not rented
5. Not have a single owner hold title to more than 10 percent of the units in the project

In addition, the lender will need to confirm that the homeowners association has a sufficiently strong balance sheet, insurance, and no significant deferred maintenance. Even if the condominium project meets these requirements, only 10 percent of the units in a development can be approved for FHA-insured loans. Proprietary reverse mortgage products often have looser standards for condominiums.

Excess Land

It is hard to imagine having too much land, but HUD is not interested in being a landowner and will not include excess land in a reverse mortgage. HUD defines excess land as that which is larger than what is typical for the neighborhood and capable of a separate use. This usually means it could be subdivided into a separate legal parcel. If you own more than five acres, it is likely that any property beyond five acres will not be included in the appraised value of your property for the purpose of the reverse mortgage.

Also, if you have a reverse mortgage, you may be restricted in what you can do with the excess land. You will not be able to subdivide the property without first paying off the reverse mortgage loan. Said another way, subdividing and selling the subdivided parcel will trigger repayment, because you are changing title to the property. So, if you have excess land and live in an area where subdivision makes economic sense, you may want to subdivide your property prior to obtaining a reverse mortgage. Besides, the money you make from subdividing could delay or eliminate your need for a reverse mortgage.

Manufactured and Modular Homes

It is easy to confuse a manufactured home and a modular home. A manufactured home is a complete unit with all its systems—for example, electrical and plumbing—installed prior to delivery to its site. To be eligible for a HECM, the manufactured homes must:

- Be built after June 15, 1976
- Comply with the Manufactured Home Construction and Safety Standards
- Be classified as real estate for tax purposes
- Have not been installed in another site prior to its current site
- Be at least 400 square feet
- Have a permanent foundation that meets HUD guidelines
- Have its axles and tongues removed
- Have permanent utilities installed
- Have a permanent skirt around the perimeter

Even if these criteria are satisfied, a manufactured home will not be eligible if it is located in a cooperative housing development or qualifies for HUD's Special Risk Insurance Fund. Mobile homes are not eligible, because they do not have a permanent foundation with axles and tongues removed.

Modular homes, on the other hand, are partially prefabricated in a factory, but the electrical and plumbing systems are added on site. When a modular unit is completely assembled on site, it becomes permanently fixed to the site and must comply with local building codes. Modular homes are often indistinguishable from stick-built homes and, thus, are treated by HUD the same as stick-built homes. Modular homes are eligible for reverse mortgages.

Private Roads and Shared Driveways

Not surprisingly, to be eligible for a reverse mortgage a property must be accessible to both vehicle and pedestrian traffic by either a public or private road. Homes without access do not have significant market value. If a property is serviced only by a private road, it must meet the following minimal standards:

- The road must be an all-weather surface over which emergency vehicles and typical passenger vehicles can pass at all times.
- There must be a joint maintenance agreement signed by all parties that use the private road.
- Access must be established and protected by a permanent ingress/egress easement recorded in the public records.

The joint maintenance agreement must be a legally binding agreement on all of the parties and it must clearly describe the private road, including where it connects with the public road, and set out a plan for how the costs of maintaining the road are shared. In addition, the agreement must be transferable to the heirs, personal representatives, successors, and assigns of the property owners.

These requirements may be waived if the property abuts a public road and there is a common driveway easement between two property owners that is made of an all-weather surface.

Leasehold Interests

A leasehold interest exists when the borrower's right to use the property is based on a lease agreement with the owner of the land. A leasehold interest can qualify for a HECM if it meets FHA guidelines. There are two main qualifications: First, the third-party property owner must hold the property in fee simple (the most common form of ownership in the United States, which provides the owner with absolute ownership to the entire property including the right to dispose of the property during one's lifetime and to decide who receives the property after the owner's death). Second, the lease term must be sufficiently long, meaning it must:

- Be at least 99 years and renewable
- Have a remaining term of at least fifty years beyond the 100th birthday of the youngest borrower

Take a copy of the lease agreement to your first meeting with the lender, because the lender will want to review the agreement to be sure it meets FHA standards. There are also special appraisal rules for leasehold interests. Talk to a qualified appraiser for details.

Homestead Advisory

To encourage productive settlement of its broad territories, the United States granted land to people who settled and farmed public lands. Property that was acquired in this manner, instead of being purchased with cash, is known as a homestead. Homestead exemption laws protect homestead property from creditors. Homestead rights permit a spouse and children to live on the property after the head of the household dies, regardless of how the title to the property is held.

Because of this homestead right, both spouses will be required to sign a conveyance deed as part of the reverse mortgage closing even if one spouse is removed from title prior to closing. Remember from Chapter 2 that some people may be tempted to remove a younger spouse from the title in order to qualify for a reverse mortgage. This is not normally a good idea because of the risk that the loan will become due and payable at the death of the borrowing spouse, and the surviving spouse may then be forced to either refinance the loan or sell the home. For this reason, the spouse who is considering being removed is required to attend counseling to understand the risks of this action.

Wells and Septic Systems

If your property is serviced by a well and septic system rather than a public utility system, the well must meet the following requirements:

- Tested for lead, nitrate, total coliform, and fecal coliform
- Dug at least 20 feet deep with casing
- Located at least 50 feet away from the septic tank
- The well and drain field must be at least 100 feet apart
- The well must be at least 15 feet from the house and 10 feet from any lot line
- Not be shared by more than four houses

A separate septic inspection is not required unless the inspector sees signs of malfunction at the time of the usual required home inspection. In addition, the inspection must state whether public water and sewer are available. If public utilities are available, hookup is required unless the cost would exceed 3 percent of the value of the property. Finally, any shared wells or septic systems must have a recorded agreement regarding maintenance and use between all the parties.

Wood Stoves and Space Heaters

If your home is heated by a wood stove or space heater, the appraiser will check to make sure the appliances are installed properly and in good working condition. The appraiser will also determine whether the appliances meet applicable building and fire codes to ensure safety. Finally, to ensure your health, the appraiser will determine whether the wood stove or space heater is adequate to heat the house.

Estate Planning

In Chapter 8 we discussed estate planning in the broad context of your legacy and how you want to be remembered. This section discusses some of the technical aspects of estate planning that may impact your reverse mortgage; specifically, living trusts, life estates, and powers of attorney.

Living Trusts

A living trust (also called inter vivos trust) is a type of trust created to hold ownership of all or some of a person's assets during his or her life and to hold and/or distribute those assets after death. It is a widely used estate-planning tool because it can allow assets to pass to heirs without going through the court system known as probate. Avoiding probate saves time and money and maintains privacy. Living trusts are also effective for planning for incapacity. The parties to a living trust include:

- Grantor—the person who established the trust
- Trustee—the person who manages the trust assets
- Beneficiary—the person who receives trust assets or benefits from trust assets

Normally, the grantor is the original beneficiary of a living trust. Those who receive trust assets after the death of the grantor are known as the remainder beneficiaries.

HUD will originate reverse mortgages in the name of a living trust as long as certain requirements are met. The first requirement is that the loan documents must be signed by all appropriate parties. The trustee and the borrower/beneficiary must sign the mortgage or deed of trust to create a valid first lien on the property. The borrower/beneficiary must sign the promissory note and the loan agreement. The trustee is not a party to the loan agreement but may be asked to sign the promissory note.

Second, all beneficiaries of the trust must be eligible borrowers. This means that the borrower/beneficiary must occupy the property as a primary residence, and no new beneficiaries can be added. Contingent beneficiaries, who do not control the trust assets and do not receive benefits from the trust until the beneficiary is deceased, do not need to be eligible borrowers.

Finally, the lender must be satisfied that the trust agreement is valid and enforceable pursuant to applicable law and that it adequately protects the lender. To protect the lender, the trust agreement must give the lender the right to be notified of any change of occupancy and transfer of a beneficial interest. It also must be clear that all borrowers have the legal right to occupy the property during their life. In many cases, the lender will require an "opinion letter" from an attorney licensed in the state in which the borrower resides to provide these assurances.

HECM borrowers may transfer the property to a living trust after closing without causing the loan to become due and payable if the lender finds that the trust meets all the requirements that would have applied if the trust owned the property at closing. Of course, the lender may require the trust to legally assume the borrower's obligation to repay the debt.

Similarly, if the trust is terminated or the property is transferred out of the trust, the loan will not become due and payable, as long as one or more of the original borrowers who signed the note and loan agreement continue to occupy the property as a primary residence and retain title to the property.

You may also have heard of a testamentary trust. A testamentary trust arises upon the death of the person who created the trust, unlike a living trust, which exists during the grantor's life. A testamentary trust is created by a will. Property held in a testamentary trust is not eligible for a reverse mortgage, because the trust does not hold title to any assets during the life of the homeowner.

As you can see, trusts and reverse mortgages together can be complicated. That said, there are many advantages to placing your home in a living trust. Because the homeowner can be both trustee and beneficiary, he or she retains absolute control over the property as long as he or she has mental capacity. Living trusts are widely accepted by lenders, so the trust should not be a hurdle to getting a reverse mortgage. Be sure to speak with an estate-planning attorney and knowledgeable lender about the impact of a reverse mortgage on a trust, and vice versa.

Life Estate

A life estate is an interest in property that allows a person to live in a home during his or her lifetime. Upon the death of the holder of a life estate, his or her interest in the property is gone, leaving all property rights to the underlying owner of the property. On a property rights continuum, a life estate can be thought of as lying somewhere between a leasehold interest and fee simple ownership.

Most property in the United States is held in fee simple; however, life estates are sometimes used as an estate-planning tool. For example, a mother might sell her house to her son subject to a life estate. This means the mother has the right to live in the house until she dies, even though the son actually owns the house.

Properties with a life estate may be eligible for a reverse mortgage, providing the mortgage encumbers the fee simple interest in the property. This requires the borrower and all other owners of the property, including the underlying owner, to execute the mortgage or deed of trust that gives the lender a lien on the property. Only the borrower, however, is obligated to sign the promissory note and the loan agreement. Not all lenders are willing to work with life estates, so if you have one, ask about it early in the reverse mortgage process.

Power of Attorney

A power of attorney is a document that gives another person legal authority to act on your behalf. The person who gives the authority is called the principal, and the person to whom the authority is given is called an attorney-in-fact or agent. A durable power of attorney is effective upon signing, or on a specified date, and continues in effect even if you become incapacitated. A power of attorney can be drafted to not be effective until the principal is incapacitated, but most lenders will not accept this type of power of attorney because of the difficulty of proving incapacity and discerning the wishes of the principal.

HUD has guidelines for the use of a power of attorney to sign reverse mortgage documents. The power of attorney must comply with state laws regarding signatures, notarization, witnesses, and recordation. A key requirement is that the principal is capable of understanding what he is doing by signing the power of attorney. Having a notary and attorney witness the signature aids credibility. The document must also be specifically designed to survive incapacity and avoid the need for court proceedings. In other words, it must be a durable power of attorney.

Incompetent borrowers may not sign the reverse mortgage application, because they are not capable of understanding what it is they are signing. Instead, a court-appointed conservator or guardian or a person holding durable power of attorney may execute any necessary documents as long as that person supplies evidence of his or her authority to the lender. Even if a borrower is legally competent, an attorney-in-fact holding durable power of attorney may sign the reverse mortgage application on behalf of the borrower.

The powers granted in the document creating durable power of attorney can be general or limited. A general power applies to all financial and real estate matters. The power, however, can be specifically limited to the reverse mortgage transaction. If the power of attorney does not clearly limit the powers, it will be presumed to be a general power of attorney. The power of attorney itself is a fairly simple document; however, defining the powers can have far-reaching implications.

Conclusion

Home equity is one of your largest assets, so it is not surprising that tapping into this equity involves consideration of a variety of real estate, financial, and estate-planning circumstances. Luckily, there are a number of dedicated counselors, lenders, and professionals with the specialized knowledge necessary to help you make informed decisions. With the help of your reverse mortgage team, you will find a solution best suited to your circumstances.

Loan Comparison Worksheets

The sample worksheets on the following pages illustrate how available loan amounts vary between the HECM, Home Keeper, and Cash Account Advantage reverse mortgages. The loan amounts in the samples are based on estimated costs, interest rates, and loan limits as of November 2006. Monthly payment amounts are based on a tenure payment plan. These estimates assume there is no existing mortgage or other lien on the property that would need to be paid off and deducted from the total loan amount. Actual available loan amounts will vary depending on many factors, including the lender's underwriting practices, the current terms for each type of reverse mortgage, and interest rates.

Sample 4: 72-Year-Old Borrower in Scottsdale, Arizona, with a $350,000 House

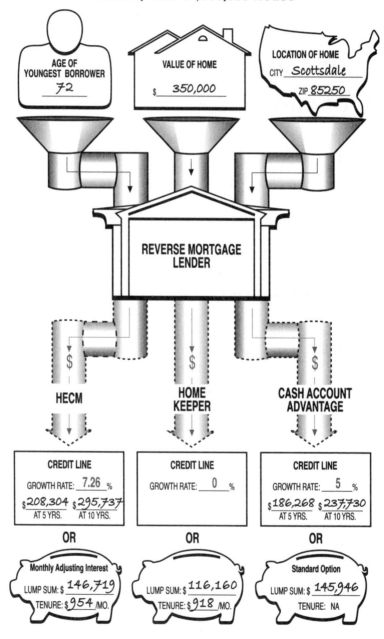

Sample 5: 72-Year-Old Borrower in Scottsdale, Arizona, with a $650,000 House

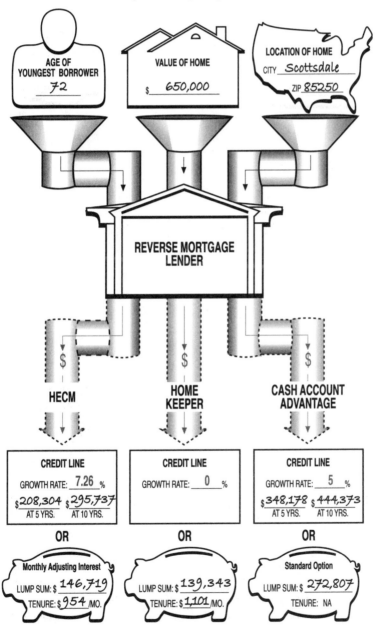

AGE OF YOUNGEST BORROWER
72

VALUE OF HOME
$ 650,000

LOCATION OF HOME
CITY Scottsdale
ZIP 85250

REVERSE MORTGAGE LENDER

HECM

HOME KEEPER

CASH ACCOUNT ADVANTAGE

CREDIT LINE
GROWTH RATE: 7.26 %
$208,304 $295,737
AT 5 YRS.   AT 10 YRS.

CREDIT LINE
GROWTH RATE: 0 %

CREDIT LINE
GROWTH RATE: 5 %
$348,178 $444,373
AT 5 YRS.   AT 10 YRS.

OR

OR

OR

Monthly Adjusting Interest
LUMP SUM: $ 146,719
TENURE: $954 /MO.

LUMP SUM: $ 139,343
TENURE: $1,101 /MO.

Standard Option
LUMP SUM: $ 272,807
TENURE: NA

Sample 6: 62-Year-Old Borrower in Scottsdale, Arizona, with a $250,000 House

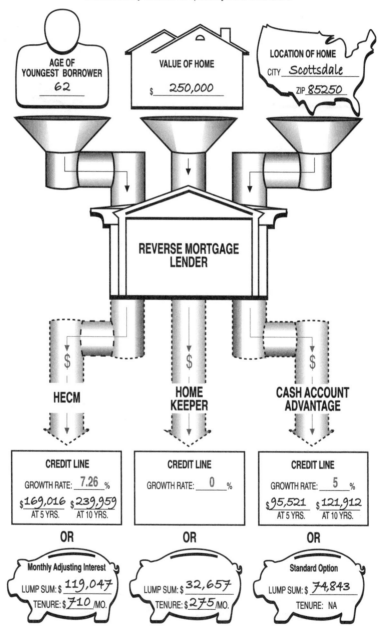

AGE OF YOUNGEST BORROWER
62

VALUE OF HOME
$ 250,000

LOCATION OF HOME
CITY Scottsdale
ZIP 85250

REVERSE MORTGAGE LENDER

HECM

HOME KEEPER

CASH ACCOUNT ADVANTAGE

CREDIT LINE
GROWTH RATE: 7.26 %
$169,016 $239,959
AT 5 YRS.   AT 10 YRS.

CREDIT LINE
GROWTH RATE: 0 %

CREDIT LINE
GROWTH RATE: 5 %
$95,521 $121,912
AT 5 YRS.   AT 10 YRS.

OR

OR

OR

Monthly Adjusting Interest
LUMP SUM: $ 119,047
TENURE: $ 710 /MO.

LUMP SUM: $ 32,657
TENURE: $ 275 /MO.

Standard Option
LUMP SUM: $ 74,843
TENURE: NA

Sample 7: 82-Year-Old Borrower in Scottsdale, Arizona, with a $250,000 House

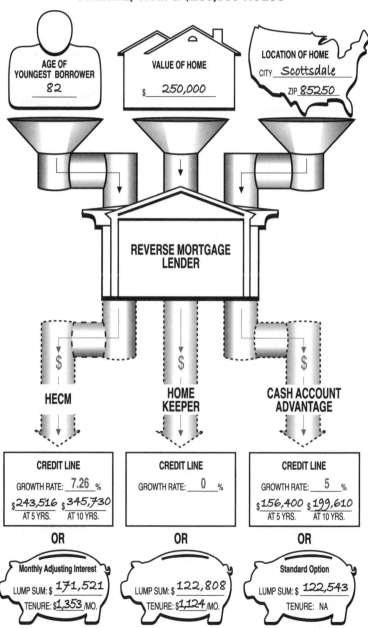

AGE OF YOUNGEST BORROWER
82

VALUE OF HOME
$ 250,000

LOCATION OF HOME
CITY Scottsdale
ZIP 85250

REVERSE MORTGAGE LENDER

HECM

HOME KEEPER

CASH ACCOUNT ADVANTAGE

CREDIT LINE	CREDIT LINE	CREDIT LINE
GROWTH RATE: 7.26 %	GROWTH RATE: 0 %	GROWTH RATE: 5 %
$243,516 AT 5 YRS. $345,730 AT 10 YRS.		$156,400 AT 5 YRS. $199,610 AT 10 YRS.

OR

OR

OR

Monthly Adjusting Interest
LUMP SUM: $ 171,521
TENURE: $1,353 /MO.

LUMP SUM: $ 122,808
TENURE: $1,124 /MO.

Standard Option
LUMP SUM: $ 122,543
TENURE: NA

Sample 8: 72-Year-Old-Borrower in Santa Barbara, California, with a $250,000 House

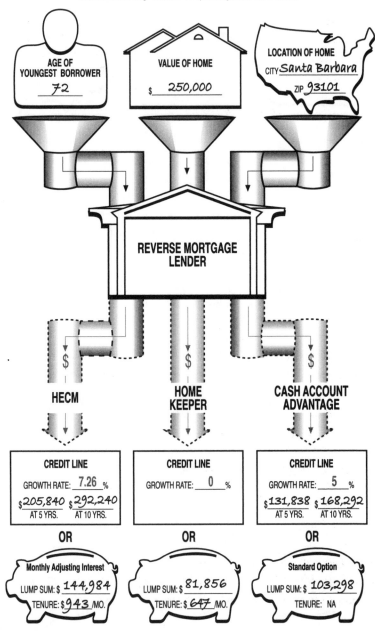

AGE OF YOUNGEST BORROWER
72

VALUE OF HOME
$ 250,000

LOCATION OF HOME
CITY Santa Barbara
ZIP 93101

REVERSE MORTGAGE LENDER

$

$

$

HECM

HOME KEEPER

CASH ACCOUNT ADVANTAGE

CREDIT LINE
GROWTH RATE: 7.26 %
$205,840 AT 5 YRS. $292,240 AT 10 YRS.

CREDIT LINE
GROWTH RATE: 0 %

CREDIT LINE
GROWTH RATE: 5 %
$131,838 AT 5 YRS. $168,292 AT 10 YRS.

OR

OR

OR

Monthly Adjusting Interest
LUMP SUM: $ 144,984
TENURE: $ 943 /MO.

LUMP SUM: $ 81,856
TENURE: $ 647 /MO.

Standard Option
LUMP SUM: $ 103,298
TENURE: NA

Sample 9: 72-Year-Old Borrower in Santa Barbara, California, with a $350,000 House

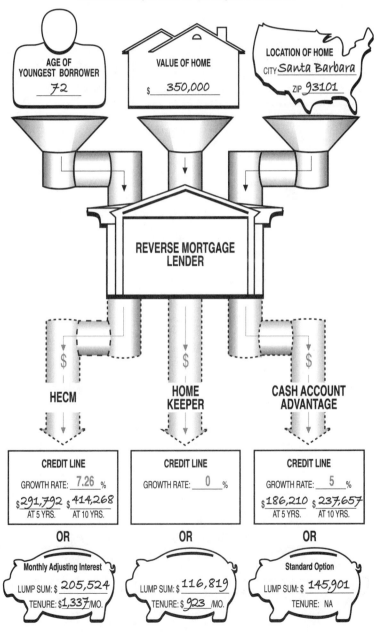

AGE OF YOUNGEST BORROWER
72

VALUE OF HOME
$ 350,000

LOCATION OF HOME
CITY Santa Barbara
ZIP 93101

REVERSE MORTGAGE LENDER

HECM

HOME KEEPER

CASH ACCOUNT ADVANTAGE

CREDIT LINE
GROWTH RATE: 7.26 %
$291,792 AT 5 YRS. $414,268 AT 10 YRS.

CREDIT LINE
GROWTH RATE: 0 %

CREDIT LINE
GROWTH RATE: 5 %
$186,210 AT 5 YRS. $237,657 AT 10 YRS.

OR

OR

OR

Monthly Adjusting Interest
LUMP SUM: $ 205,524
TENURE: $1,337 /MO.

LUMP SUM: $ 116,819
TENURE: $ 923 /MO.

Standard Option
LUMP SUM: $ 145,901
TENURE: NA

Sample 10: 62-Year-Old Borrower in Santa Barbara, California, with a $250,000 House

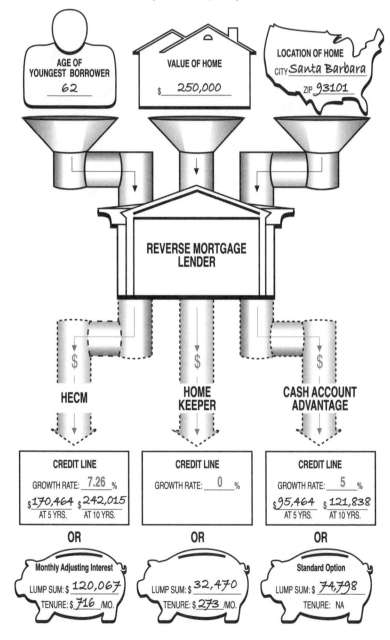

Sample 11: 82-Year-Old Borrower in Santa Barbara, California, with a $250,000 House

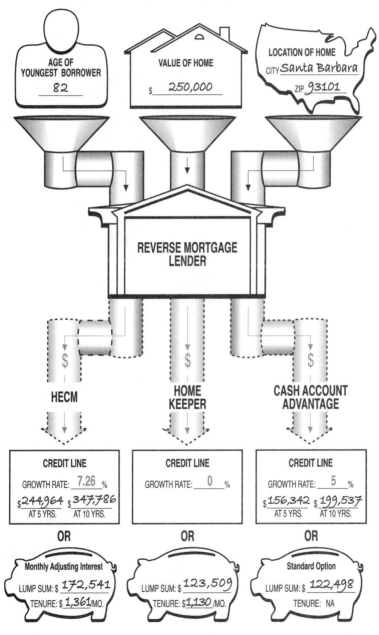

AGE OF YOUNGEST BORROWER
82

VALUE OF HOME
$ 250,000

LOCATION OF HOME
CITY Santa Barbara
ZIP 93101

REVERSE MORTGAGE LENDER

$

$

$

HECM

HOME KEEPER

CASH ACCOUNT ADVANTAGE

CREDIT LINE	CREDIT LINE	CREDIT LINE
GROWTH RATE: 7.26 %	GROWTH RATE: 0 %	GROWTH RATE: 5 %
$244,964 $347,786		$156,342 $199,537
AT 5 YRS. AT 10 YRS.		AT 5 YRS. AT 10 YRS.

OR

OR

OR

Monthly Adjusting Interest
LUMP SUM: $ 172,541
TENURE: $ 1,361/MO.

LUMP SUM: $ 123,509
TENURE: $ 1,130 /MO.

Standard Option
LUMP SUM: $ 122,498
TENURE: NA

Sample 12: 72-Year-Old Borrower in New York City, with a $250,000 House

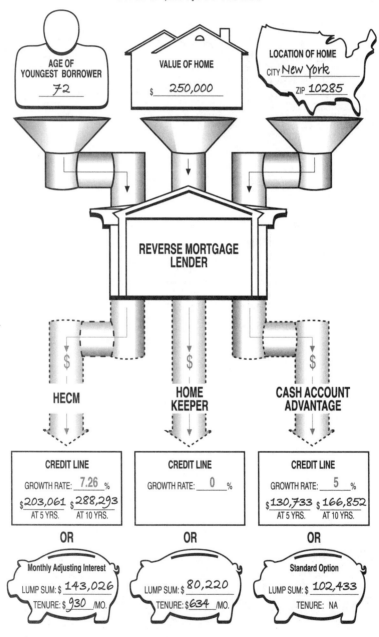

AGE OF YOUNGEST BORROWER
72

VALUE OF HOME
$ **250,000**

LOCATION OF HOME
CITY **New York**
ZIP **10285**

REVERSE MORTGAGE LENDER

HECM

HOME KEEPER

CASH ACCOUNT ADVANTAGE

CREDIT LINE		CREDIT LINE	CREDIT LINE	
GROWTH RATE: **7.26** %		GROWTH RATE: **0** %	GROWTH RATE: **5** %	
$**203,061** AT 5 YRS.	$**288,293** AT 10 YRS.		$**130,733** AT 5 YRS.	$**166,852** AT 10 YRS.

OR

OR

OR

Monthly Adjusting Interest
LUMP SUM: $ **143,026**
TENURE: $ **930** /MO.

LUMP SUM: $ **80,220**
TENURE: $ **634** /MO.

Standard Option
LUMP SUM: $ **102,433**
TENURE: NA

Sample 13: 72-Year-Old Borrower in New York City, with a $350,000 House

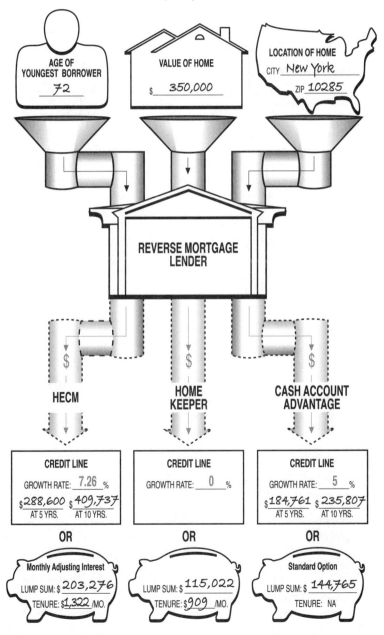

AGE OF YOUNGEST BORROWER
72

VALUE OF HOME
$ 350,000

LOCATION OF HOME
CITY New York
ZIP 10285

REVERSE MORTGAGE LENDER

HECM

HOME KEEPER

CASH ACCOUNT ADVANTAGE

CREDIT LINE
GROWTH RATE: 7.26 %
$288,600 $409,737
AT 5 YRS.   AT 10 YRS.

CREDIT LINE
GROWTH RATE: 0 %

CREDIT LINE
GROWTH RATE: 5 %
$184,761 $235,807
AT 5 YRS.   AT 10 YRS.

OR

OR

OR

Monthly Adjusting Interest
LUMP SUM: $ 203,276
TENURE: $1,322 /MO.

LUMP SUM: $ 115,022
TENURE: $909 /MO.

Standard Option
LUMP SUM: $ 144,765
TENURE: NA

Sample 14: 72-Year-Old Borrower in New York City, with a $650,000 House

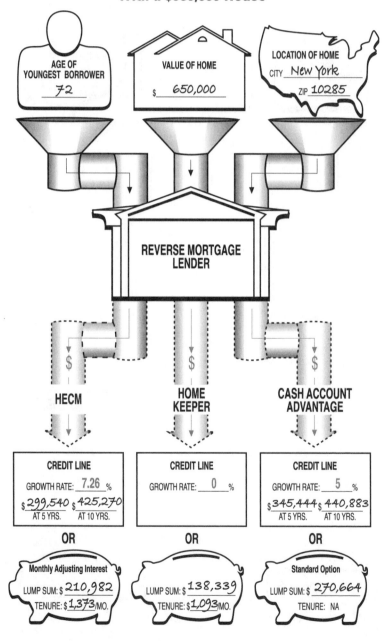

AGE OF YOUNGEST BORROWER
72

VALUE OF HOME
$ 650,000

LOCATION OF HOME
CITY New York
ZIP 10285

REVERSE MORTGAGE LENDER

$

$

$

HECM

HOME KEEPER

CASH ACCOUNT ADVANTAGE

CREDIT LINE	CREDIT LINE	CREDIT LINE
GROWTH RATE: 7.26 %	GROWTH RATE: 0 %	GROWTH RATE: 5 %
$299,540 AT 5 YRS. $425,270 AT 10 YRS.		$345,444 AT 5 YRS. $440,883 AT 10 YRS.

OR

OR

OR

Monthly Adjusting Interest
LUMP SUM: $ 210,982
TENURE: $ 1,373/MO.

LUMP SUM: $ 138,339
TENURE: $ 1,093/MO.

Standard Option
LUMP SUM: $ 270,664
TENURE: NA

Sample 15: 62-Year-Old Borrower in New York City, with a $250,000 House

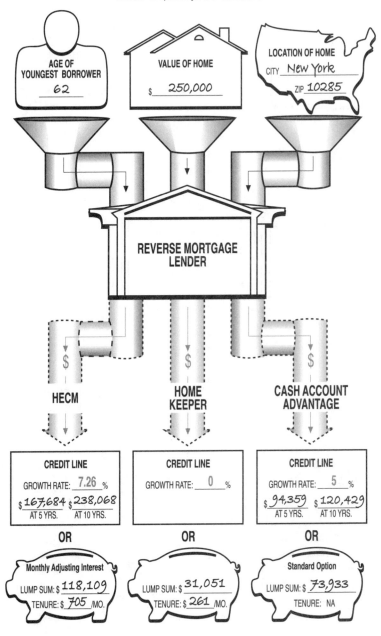

AGE OF YOUNGEST BORROWER
62

VALUE OF HOME
$ 250,000

LOCATION OF HOME
CITY New York
ZIP 10285

REVERSE MORTGAGE LENDER

HECM

HOME KEEPER

CASH ACCOUNT ADVANTAGE

CREDIT LINE
GROWTH RATE: 7.26 %
$ 167,684 $ 238,068
AT 5 YRS.   AT 10 YRS.

CREDIT LINE
GROWTH RATE: 0 %

CREDIT LINE
GROWTH RATE: 5 %
$ 94,359 $ 120,429
AT 5 YRS.   AT 10 YRS.

OR

OR

OR

Monthly Adjusting Interest
LUMP SUM: $ 118,109
TENURE: $ 705 /MO.

LUMP SUM: $ 31,051
TENURE: $ 261 /MO.

Standard Option
LUMP SUM: $ 73,933
TENURE: NA

Sample 16: 82-Year-Old Borrower in New York City, with a $250,000 House

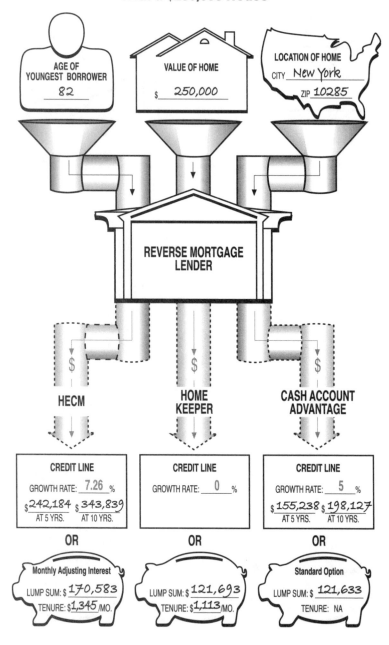

AGE OF YOUNGEST BORROWER
82

VALUE OF HOME
$ 250,000

LOCATION OF HOME
CITY New York
ZIP 10285

REVERSE MORTGAGE LENDER

HECM

HOME KEEPER

CASH ACCOUNT ADVANTAGE

CREDIT LINE

GROWTH RATE: 7.26 %

$242,184 $343,839
AT 5 YRS. AT 10 YRS.

CREDIT LINE

GROWTH RATE: 0 %

CREDIT LINE

GROWTH RATE: 5 %

$155,238 $198,127
AT 5 YRS. AT 10 YRS.

OR

OR

OR

Monthly Adjusting Interest

LUMP SUM: $ 170,583

TENURE: $1,345 /MO.

LUMP SUM: $ 121,693

TENURE: $1,113 /MO.

Standard Option

LUMP SUM: $ 121,633

TENURE: NA

Sample 17: 72-Year-Old Borrower in Colorado Springs, Colorado, with a $250,000 House

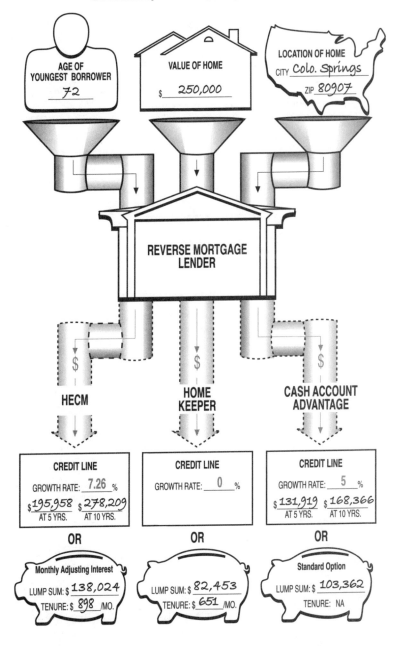

AGE OF YOUNGEST BORROWER
72

VALUE OF HOME
$ 250,000

LOCATION OF HOME
CITY Colo. Springs
ZIP 80907

REVERSE MORTGAGE LENDER

HECM

HOME KEEPER

CASH ACCOUNT ADVANTAGE

CREDIT LINE	CREDIT LINE	CREDIT LINE
GROWTH RATE: 7.26 %	GROWTH RATE: 0 %	GROWTH RATE: 5 %
$195,958 AT 5 YRS. $278,209 AT 10 YRS.		$131,919 AT 5 YRS. $168,366 AT 10 YRS.

OR

OR

OR

Monthly Adjusting Interest
LUMP SUM: $ 138,024
TENURE: $ 898 /MO.

LUMP SUM: $ 82,453
TENURE: $ 651 /MO.

Standard Option
LUMP SUM: $ 103,362
TENURE: NA

Sample 18: 72-Year-Old Borrower in Colorado Springs, Colorado, with a $650,000 House

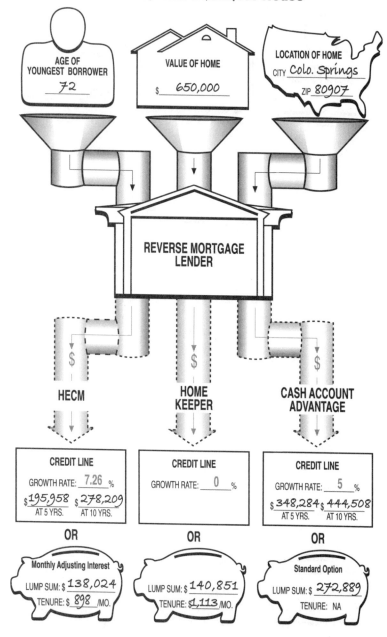

AGE OF YOUNGEST BORROWER
72

VALUE OF HOME
$ 650,000

LOCATION OF HOME
CITY Colo. Springs
ZIP 80907

REVERSE MORTGAGE LENDER

HECM

HOME KEEPER

CASH ACCOUNT ADVANTAGE

CREDIT LINE
GROWTH RATE: 7.26 %
$195,958 AT 5 YRS. $278,209 AT 10 YRS.

CREDIT LINE
GROWTH RATE: 0 %

CREDIT LINE
GROWTH RATE: 5 %
$348,284 AT 5 YRS. $444,508 AT 10 YRS.

OR

OR

OR

Monthly Adjusting Interest
LUMP SUM: $ 138,024
TENURE: $ 898 /MO.

LUMP SUM: $ 140,851
TENURE: $1,113 /MO.

Standard Option
LUMP SUM: $ 272,889
TENURE: NA

Sample 19: 62-Year-Old Borrower in Colorado Springs, Colorado, with a $250,000 House

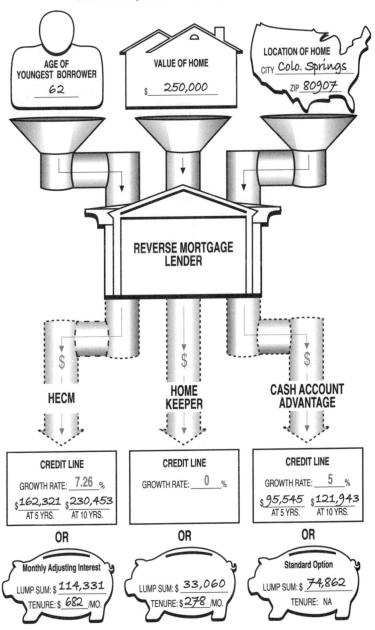

AGE OF YOUNGEST BORROWER
62

VALUE OF HOME
$ 250,000

LOCATION OF HOME
CITY Colo. Springs
ZIP 80907

REVERSE MORTGAGE LENDER

HECM

HOME KEEPER

CASH ACCOUNT ADVANTAGE

CREDIT LINE	CREDIT LINE	CREDIT LINE
GROWTH RATE: 7.26 %	GROWTH RATE: 0 %	GROWTH RATE: 5 %
$162,321 AT 5 YRS. $230,453 AT 10 YRS.		$95,545 AT 5 YRS. $121,943 AT 10 YRS.

OR

OR

OR

Monthly Adjusting Interest
LUMP SUM: $ 114,331
TENURE: $ 682 /MO.

LUMP SUM: $ 33,060
TENURE: $ 278 /MO.

Standard Option
LUMP SUM: $ 74,862
TENURE: NA

Sample 20: 82-Year-Old Borrower in Colorado Springs, Colorado, with a $250,000 House

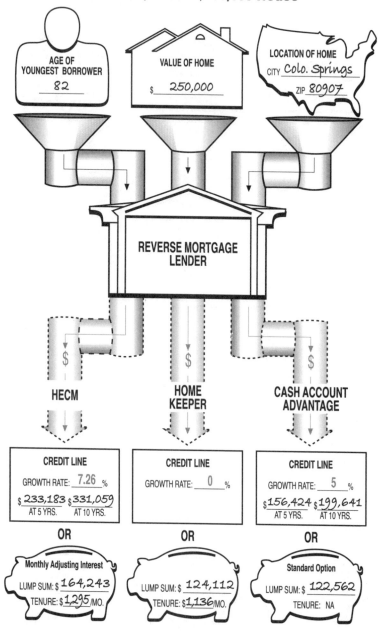

AGE OF YOUNGEST BORROWER
82

VALUE OF HOME
$ 250,000

LOCATION OF HOME
CITY Colo. Springs
ZIP 80907

REVERSE MORTGAGE LENDER

HECM

HOME KEEPER

CASH ACCOUNT ADVANTAGE

CREDIT LINE
GROWTH RATE: 7.26 %
$ 233,183 AT 5 YRS. $ 331,059 AT 10 YRS.

CREDIT LINE
GROWTH RATE: 0 %

CREDIT LINE
GROWTH RATE: 5 %
$ 156,424 AT 5 YRS. $ 199,641 AT 10 YRS.

OR

OR

OR

Monthly Adjusting Interest
LUMP SUM: $ 164,243
TENURE: $ 1,295 /MO.

LUMP SUM: $ 124,112
TENURE: $ 1,136 /MO.

Standard Option
LUMP SUM: $ 122,562
TENURE: NA

Sample 21: 72-Year-Old Borrower in Monmouth, Illinois, with a $250,000 House

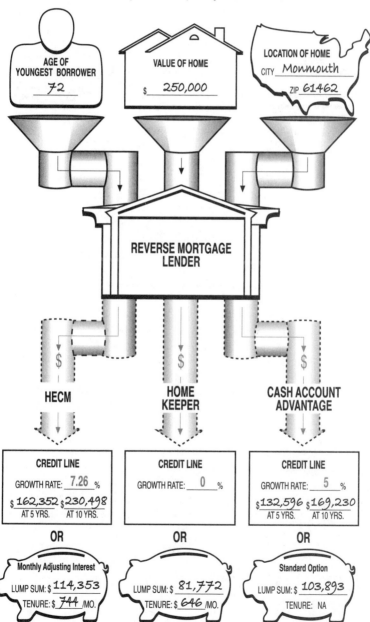

AGE OF YOUNGEST BORROWER
72

VALUE OF HOME
$ 250,000

LOCATION OF HOME
CITY Monmouth
ZIP 61462

REVERSE MORTGAGE LENDER

$

$

$

HECM

HOME KEEPER

CASH ACCOUNT ADVANTAGE

CREDIT LINE

GROWTH RATE: 7.26 %

$ 162,352 $ 230,498
AT 5 YRS.   AT 10 YRS.

CREDIT LINE

GROWTH RATE: 0 %

CREDIT LINE

GROWTH RATE: 5 %

$ 132,596 $ 169,230
AT 5 YRS.   AT 10 YRS.

OR

OR

OR

Monthly Adjusting Interest
LUMP SUM: $ 114,353
TENURE: $ 744 /MO.

LUMP SUM: $ 81,772
TENURE: $ 646 /MO.

Standard Option
LUMP SUM: $ 103,893
TENURE: NA

Sample 22: 72-Year-Old Borrower in Monmouth, Illinois, with a $350,000 House

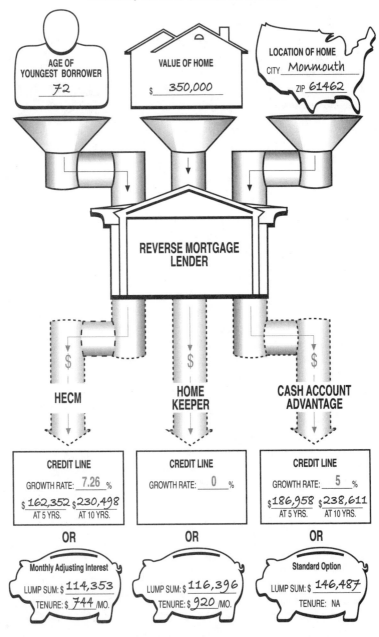

AGE OF YOUNGEST BORROWER
72

VALUE OF HOME
$ 350,000

LOCATION OF HOME
CITY Monmouth
ZIP 61462

REVERSE MORTGAGE LENDER

HECM

HOME KEEPER

CASH ACCOUNT ADVANTAGE

CREDIT LINE	CREDIT LINE	CREDIT LINE
GROWTH RATE: 7.26 %	GROWTH RATE: 0 %	GROWTH RATE: 5 %
$ 162,352 AT 5 YRS. $ 230,498 AT 10 YRS.		$ 186,958 AT 5 YRS. $ 238,611 AT 10 YRS.

OR

OR

OR

Monthly Adjusting Interest
LUMP SUM: $ 114,353
TENURE: $ 744 /MO.

LUMP SUM: $ 116,396
TENURE: $ 920 /MO.

Standard Option
LUMP SUM: $ 146,487
TENURE: NA

Sample 23: 72-Year-Old Borrower in Monmouth, Illinois, with a $650,000 House

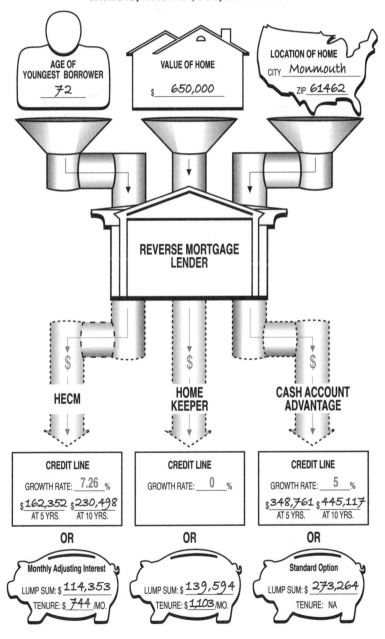

AGE OF YOUNGEST BORROWER
72

VALUE OF HOME
$ 650,000

LOCATION OF HOME
CITY Monmouth
ZIP 61462

REVERSE MORTGAGE LENDER

HECM	HOME KEEPER	CASH ACCOUNT ADVANTAGE

CREDIT LINE	CREDIT LINE	CREDIT LINE
GROWTH RATE: 7.26 %	GROWTH RATE: 0 %	GROWTH RATE: 5 %
$162,352 AT 5 YRS. $230,498 AT 10 YRS.		$348,761 AT 5 YRS. $445,117 AT 10 YRS.

OR — OR — OR

Monthly Adjusting Interest
LUMP SUM: $ 114,353
TENURE: $ 744 /MO.

LUMP SUM: $ 139,594
TENURE: $ 1,103 /MO.

Standard Option
LUMP SUM: $ 273,264
TENURE: NA

Sample 24: 62-Year-Old Borrower in Monmouth, Illinois, with a $250,000 House

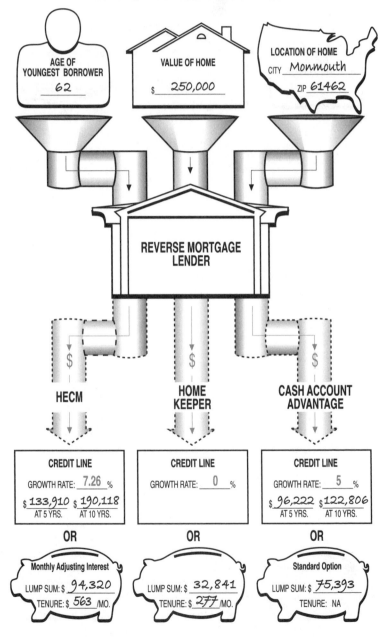

AGE OF YOUNGEST BORROWER
62

VALUE OF HOME
$ 250,000

LOCATION OF HOME
CITY Monmouth
ZIP 61462

REVERSE MORTGAGE LENDER

$

$

$

HECM

HOME KEEPER

CASH ACCOUNT ADVANTAGE

CREDIT LINE	CREDIT LINE	CREDIT LINE
GROWTH RATE: 7.26 %	GROWTH RATE: 0 %	GROWTH RATE: 5 %
$ 133,910 $ 190,118		$ 96,222 $122,806
AT 5 YRS. AT 10 YRS.		AT 5 YRS. AT 10 YRS.

OR

OR

OR

Monthly Adjusting Interest
LUMP SUM: $ 94,320
TENURE: $ 563 /MO.

LUMP SUM: $ 32,841
TENURE: $ 277 /MO.

Standard Option
LUMP SUM: $ 75,393
TENURE: NA

Sample 25: 82-Year-Old Borrower in Monmouth, Illinois, with a $250,000 House

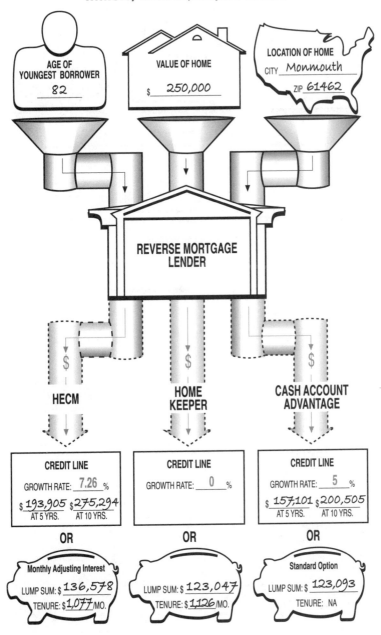

AGE OF YOUNGEST BORROWER
82

VALUE OF HOME
$ 250,000

LOCATION OF HOME
CITY Monmouth
ZIP 61462

REVERSE MORTGAGE LENDER

$

$

$

HECM

HOME KEEPER

CASH ACCOUNT ADVANTAGE

CREDIT LINE
GROWTH RATE: 7.26 %
$ 193,905 $ 275,294
AT 5 YRS. AT 10 YRS.

CREDIT LINE
GROWTH RATE: 0 %

CREDIT LINE
GROWTH RATE: 5 %
$ 157,101 $ 200,505
AT 5 YRS. AT 10 YRS.

OR

OR

OR

Monthly Adjusting Interest
LUMP SUM: $ 136,578
TENURE: $ 1,077 /MO.

LUMP SUM: $ 123,047
TENURE: $ 1,126 /MO.

Standard Option
LUMP SUM: $ 123,093
TENURE: NA

Personal Reverse Mortgage Comparison Worksheet

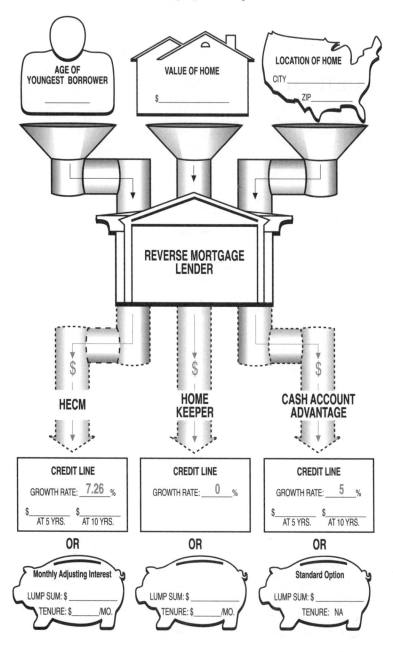

Loan-Specific Worksheets

HECM Worksheet

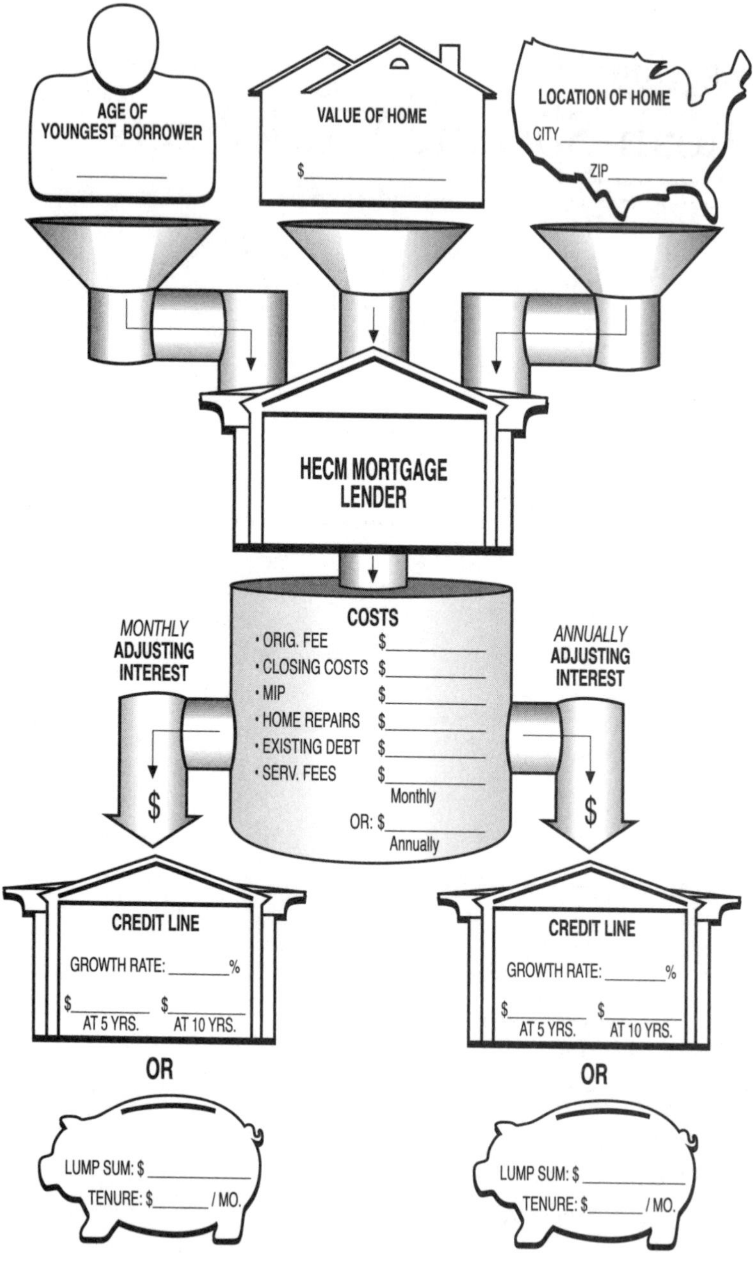

AGE OF YOUNGEST BORROWER

_____

VALUE OF HOME

$ _____

LOCATION OF HOME

CITY _____

ZIP _____

HECM MORTGAGE LENDER

MONTHLY **ADJUSTING INTEREST**

ANNUALLY **ADJUSTING INTEREST**

COSTS

- ORIG. FEE $ _____
- CLOSING COSTS $ _____
- MIP $ _____
- HOME REPAIRS $ _____
- EXISTING DEBT $ _____
- SERV. FEES $ _____

Monthly

OR: $ _____

Annually

$

$

CREDIT LINE

GROWTH RATE: _____ %

$ _____ $ _____

AT 5 YRS. AT 10 YRS.

OR

LUMP SUM: $ _____

TENURE: $ _____ / MO.

CREDIT LINE

GROWTH RATE: _____ %

$ _____ $ _____

AT 5 YRS. AT 10 YRS.

OR

LUMP SUM: $ _____

TENURE: $ _____ / MO.

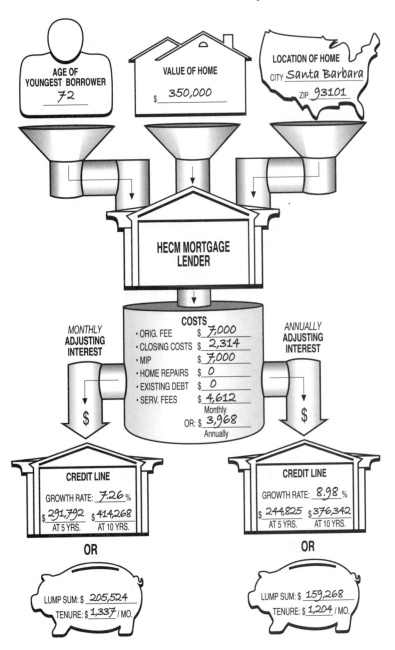

HECM Worksheet Sample

AGE OF YOUNGEST BORROWER
72

VALUE OF HOME
$ 350,000

LOCATION OF HOME
CITY Santa Barbara
ZIP 93101

HECM MORTGAGE LENDER

COSTS
- ORIG. FEE $ 7,000
- CLOSING COSTS $ 2,314
- MIP $ 7,000
- HOME REPAIRS $ 0
- EXISTING DEBT $ 0
- SERV. FEES $ 4,612 Monthly
- OR: $ 3,968 Annually

MONTHLY **ADJUSTING INTEREST**

ANNUALLY **ADJUSTING INTEREST**

CREDIT LINE
GROWTH RATE: 7.26 %
$ 291,792 $ 414,268
AT 5 YRS.   AT 10 YRS.

OR

LUMP SUM: $ 205,524
TENURE: $ 1,337 / MO.

CREDIT LINE
GROWTH RATE: 8.98 %
$ 244,825 $ 376,342
AT 5 YRS.   AT 10 YRS.

OR

LUMP SUM: $ 159,268
TENURE: $ 1,204 / MO.

Fannie Mae Home Keeper Worksheet

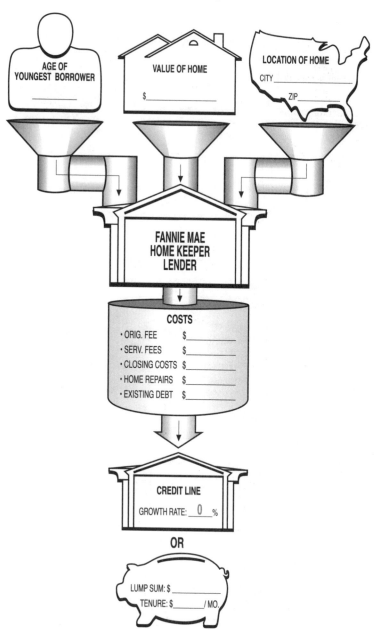

Fannie Mae Home Keeper Worksheet Sample

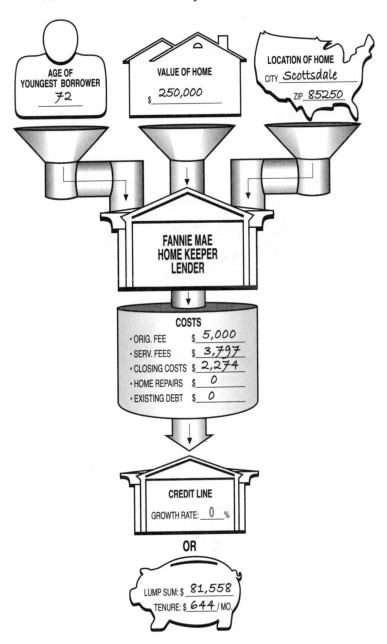

AGE OF YOUNGEST BORROWER
72

VALUE OF HOME
$ 250,000

LOCATION OF HOME
CITY Scottsdale
ZIP 85250

FANNIE MAE HOME KEEPER LENDER

COSTS
- ORIG. FEE $ 5,000
- SERV. FEES $ 3,797
- CLOSING COSTS $ 2,274
- HOME REPAIRS $ 0
- EXISTING DEBT $ 0

CREDIT LINE
GROWTH RATE: 0 %

OR

LUMP SUM: $ 81,558
TENURE: $ 644 / MO.

Cash Account Advantage Worksheet

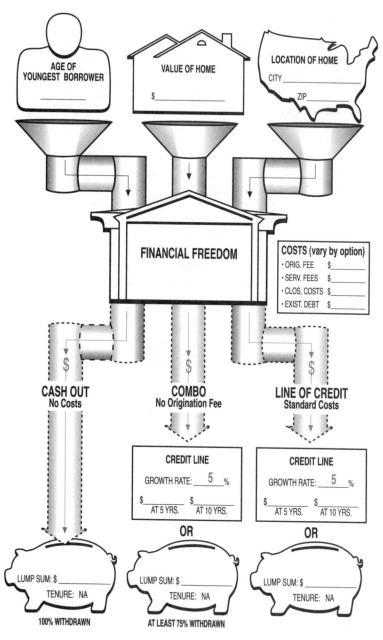

AGE OF YOUNGEST BORROWER

VALUE OF HOME

$

LOCATION OF HOME

CITY

ZIP

FINANCIAL FREEDOM

COSTS (vary by option)
- ORIG. FEE $
- SERV. FEES $
- CLOS. COSTS $
- EXIST. DEBT $

CASH OUT
No Costs

COMBO
No Origination Fee

LINE OF CREDIT
Standard Costs

CREDIT LINE

GROWTH RATE: 5 %

$_____ $_____
AT 5 YRS.   AT 10 YRS.

OR

CREDIT LINE

GROWTH RATE: 5 %

$_____ $_____
AT 5 YRS.   AT 10 YRS.

OR

LUMP SUM: $

TENURE: NA

100% WITHDRAWN

LUMP SUM: $

TENURE: NA

AT LEAST 75% WITHDRAWN

LUMP SUM: $

TENURE: NA

Cash Account Advantage Worksheet Sample

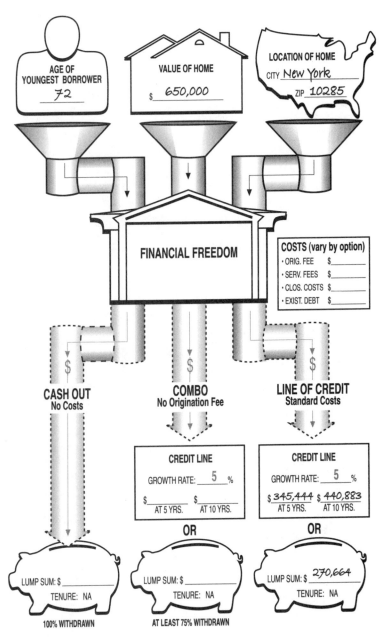

AGE OF YOUNGEST BORROWER
72

VALUE OF HOME
$ 650,000

LOCATION OF HOME
CITY New York
ZIP 10285

FINANCIAL FREEDOM

COSTS (vary by option)
- ORIG. FEE $_____
- SERV. FEES $_____
- CLOS. COSTS $_____
- EXIST. DEBT $_____

CASH OUT
No Costs

COMBO
No Origination Fee

LINE OF CREDIT
Standard Costs

CREDIT LINE
GROWTH RATE: 5 %
$_____ $_____
AT 5 YRS.   AT 10 YRS.

CREDIT LINE
GROWTH RATE: 5 %
$ 345,444 $ 440,883
AT 5 YRS.   AT 10 YRS.

OR

OR

LUMP SUM: $_____
TENURE: NA

LUMP SUM: $_____
TENURE: NA

LUMP SUM: $ 270,664
TENURE: NA

100% WITHDRAWN

AT LEAST 75% WITHDRAWN

Resources

Reverse Mortgage Resources

AARP (American Association of Retired Persons)
601 E. Street NW
Washington, DC 20049
(888) 687-2277
www.aarp.org/money/revmort

The AARP has many helpful articles and resources to help you evaluate a reverse mortgage. Its Web site includes a reverse mortgage calculator and many articles about counseling, consumers' experiences with reverse mortgages, and booklets you can either order or download free.

Administration on Aging (AOA)
Washington, DC 20201
(202) 619-0724
(888) 677-1116
www.aoa.dhhs.gov

The AOA Web site has numerous links to other Web sites related to reverse mortgages, government programs (such as Medicare and Social Security), and estate planning.

Fannie Mae
3900 Wisconsin Avenue, NW
Washington, DC 20016-2892
(800) 732-6643
www.fanniemae.com

Fannie Mae's Web site has lots of helpful reverse mortgage information including a list of reverse mortgage lenders and reverse mortgage fact sheets. Fannie Mae also has a consumer reverse mortgage guide called *Money From Home.*

Federal Trade Commission (FTC)
Consumer Response Center
600 Pennsylvania Avenue
Washington, DC 20580
(877) FTC-HELP
www.ftc.gov

The FTC has many useful consumer fact sheets, as well as a publication titled *Reverse Mortgages: Proceed with Care* and alerts about scams that may involve reverse mortgages; all are available to the public.

Financial Freedom Senior Funding Corporation
1 Banting
Irvine, CA 92618
(888) 738-3773
www.financialfreedom.com

Financial Freedom's Web site is easy to use and offers numerous pages of assistance and information about the three most popular reverse mortgages. It also offers a video about reverse mortgages.

National Council on Aging (NCOA)
1901 L Street, NW, 4th Floor
Washington, DC 20036
(202) 479-1200
www.ncoa.org

An excellent general resource for seniors. The NCOA offers several helpful booklets, such as *Use Your Home to Stay at Home: A Planning Guide for Older Consumers; Use Your Home to Stay at Home: A User's Guide for Seniors Who Need Help Now;* and a report titled *Use Your Home to Stay at Home: Expanding the Use of Reverse Mortgages to Pay for Long-Term Care.* These are available either as a download or as a booklet that can be mailed to you. NCOA also sponsors the Web site *www.benefits checkup.org,* which helps connect seniors to private and government programs that may help them pay for prescription drugs, health care, utilities, and other needs.

National Reverse Mortgage Lenders Association (NRMLA)
1400 16th Street, NW
Suite 420
Washington, DC 20036
(202) 939-1760
www.reversemortgage.org

The NRMLA, a trade association of reverse mortgage lenders, has helped establish best practice standards and a code of conduct for participating reverse mortgage lenders.

U.S. Department of Housing and Urban Development (HUD)
451 7th Street, SW
Washington, DC 20410
(202) 708-1112
www.hud.gov

HUD offers booklets and downloads, such as *Reverse Mortgages—Top Ten Things To Know,* as well as lists of counselors and fact sheets available for the public. It is also the organization to contact if you need technical information about the HECM program.

Top Three Reverse Mortgage Lenders

Financial Freedom Senior Funding Corp.
1 Banting
Irvine, CA 92618
(888) 738-3773
www.financialfreedom.com
E-mail: *sales@financialfreedom.com*

Seattle Mortgage Co.
601 108th Avenue NE, Suite 700
Bellevue, WA 98004
(800) 233-4601
www.seattlemortgage.com
E-mail: *inquiry@smcreverse.com*

Wells Fargo Home Mortgage
P.O. Box 10335
Des Moines, IA 50306-0335
(877) 937-9357
www.reversemortgages.net

Other Helpful Resources

ElderLawAnswers
535 Boylston St., 8th Floor
Boston, MA 02116-3720
(866) 267-0947
www.ElderLawAnswers.com

A Web site with information on estate planning, retirement planning, and other elder law issues.

Office of Citizen Services and Communications
U.S. General Services Administration
1800 F Street, NW
Washington, DC 20405
www.seniors.gov

This Web site offers links and information about many types of services available to seniors, including consumer protection, estate planning, and tax and financial information relating to seniors.

Pharmaceutical Research and Manufacturers of America (PhRMA)
1100 Fifteenth Street, NW
Washington, DC 20005
(800) 762-4636
www.pparx.org

PhRMA is a Web-based resource that helps low-income patients find programs to obtain low-cost or free medications. It includes both government resources and private resources for assistance. You may fill out an application online or call for a listing of programs.

Rural Housing Service National Office
U.S. Department of Agriculture
P.O. Box 66889
St. Louis, MO 63166
(800) 414-1226
www.rurdev.usda.gov

The Rural Development and Housing Facilities Program offers information and programs for home repair and renovation with low-interest loans and grants to eligible applicants.

Social Security Administration
(800) 772-1213
www.ssa.gov

The Social Security Administration Web site has information about benefits available, calculating possible benefits, and online applications. Seniors may wish to go to their local office, which they can locate on the Web site, or call the main number for assistance in locating their local office.

U.S. Department of Energy
1000 Independence Avenue, SW
Washington, DC 20585
www.eere.energy.gov/weatherization

Check the U.S. Department of Energy's Web site for programs offering assistance to low-income families with weatherization of their homes. This Web site can guide you to the local office to receive assistance, or you may apply online.

U.S. Department of Health and Human Services
Administration for Children & Families
Low Income Energy Assistance Program
370 L'Enfant Promenade, SW
Washington, DC 20447
(202) 401-9351
www.acf.hhs.gov

The U.S. Department of Health and Human Services can refer you to a regional department that may provide programs to assist low-income families with winter home-heating costs, weatherization, and energy repairs (such as furnace repair). Your local utility company may also be able to direct you to programs that provide this type of assistance.

Glossary

203b limit

The maximum loan amount a lender would be willing to lend on a federally insured HECM reverse mortgage for a qualifying home in a particular county. 203b refers to a section of the National Housing Act that establishes this limit, which varies from county to county and is updated from time to time based on current housing prices. The 2006 limit ranges from $172,632 in rural counties to $312,895 in urban counties and/or counties with higher-priced homes.

Acceleration clause

A loan provision giving the lender the right to declare the entire outstanding loan amount immediately due and payable upon the violation of a specific loan condition; for example, permanently moving out of a home for which there is a reverse mortgage. Other defaults that may cause acceleration include failure to pay property taxes or maintain homeowners insurance.

Adjustable-rate mortgage (ARM)

A mortgage loan that allows the interest rate to change at specific intervals over the course of the loan. The reverse mortgages discussed in this book are generally adjustable-rate mortgages. HECM loans allow the borrower to select an annual or semiannual interest rate adjustment.

Adjusted home value

The lower of a home's appraised value and the current loan limit for that loan as established by Fannie Mae.

Annuity

A series of equal or nearly equal periodic payments. Discussed in the context of financial planning, it generally refers to a contract sold by an insurance company and a capital investment that provides minimum payments over a specified period of time. Payments typically begin after the annuity holder retires.

Appraisal

A professional opinion or estimate of the value of a property. The appraised value of a property is the most likely price a buyer would pay and a seller would receive, assuming a willing buyer and a willing seller—neither being under compulsion to buy or sell and both having reasonable knowledge of all the relevant facts. Appraisals are usually performed using one or more of the following three methods: cost of replacement, value as a function of income produced by property, and market comparison with similar properties.

Appreciation

An increase in the value of a property. Appreciation can result from inflation, demand pressures (for example, more buyers than sellers in a particular area), or improvements and modernizations made to a home. Appreciation translates into more equity for the homeowner. With a reverse mortgage, this could ultimately mean more value to pass on to the borrower's heirs.

Area Agency on Aging (AAA)
A nonprofit organization that provides information on services and programs for older adults. AAA operates locally and nationally.

Attorney-in-fact
One who is authorized to act for another under a power of attorney, which may be general or limited in its scope.

CAIVRS
Credit Alert Interactive Voice Response System. A credit check system developed by HUD for use by all federal agencies to check for any federal debt owed.

Cap
The maximum interest rate that can be charged on a loan. It varies for each loan. For instance, on a Home Keeper, your interest rate will never be more than 12 percent above your original rate.

Cash Account Advantage Plan
Financial Freedom's reverse mortgage, the reverse mortgage is intended for seniors with home values above the current Fannie Mae limits, but is best suited for those owning homes worth $450,000 or more. The loan is a credit line only—monthly payments are not an option.

Closing
A meeting during which the loan documents are signed and the mortgage begins, typically held at a title company's office; also referred to as *settlement*.

Closing costs
The various fees and expenses payable at the time of closing. Typically the closing costs of a reverse mortgage can be financed into the loan balance.

Co-borrower
Any other person who signs and becomes obligated on the loan with the borrower. Typically a reverse mortgage loan is due when the last remaining co-borrower moves out or dies or when the house is no longer maintained.

Comparables
Similar houses in your neighborhood that may be used by an appraiser to assist in establishing an appraised value for your home. Often referred to as *comps*.

Condemnation
A court action determining that a property is unfit for use; also, when a government takes private property for public and sometimes private use with compensation to the owner under eminent domain.

Counseling
Counseling required to obtain a reverse mortgage (*see* Counselor). Reverse mortgage counseling should be free to the potential borrower.

Counselor
In the context of a reverse mortgage, a counselor approved by HUD to counsel prospective reverse mortgage borrowers on their options, educate them about reverse mortgages, and assess whether a reverse mortgage is right for them. The counselor will provide a potential borrower a certificate stating that the borrower has received counseling; this certificate is valid for 180 days.

Credit line

A credit account that lets a borrower decide when to take money out and also how much to take out; also known as a line of credit.

Credit report

Prepared by a credit bureau; an account of the applicant's credit history.

Current interest rate

In the HECM program, the interest rate currently being charged on a loan; it equals the 1-year U.S. Treasury Security rate, plus a margin.

Deed

A written document that conveys legal title to real property. Common deeds include a general warranty deed, quit claim deed, and special warranty deed.

Deed of trust

A security interest used in many states in lieu of a mortgage. The deed of trust is recorded with the county clerk and recorder of the appropriate county as public evidence of the lender's security interest in the property.

Deferred payment loans (DPLs)

A DPL is a type of reverse mortgage, usually offered by state or local government, that gives you a loan specifically to repair or improve your home. You cannot use the loan for any other purpose, and the loan is generally much smaller than one of the three major reverse mortgage products. The loan payments are not required until some later date, as determined by the loan terms.

Department of Housing and Urban Development (HUD)

Government division that oversees the nation's housing concerns. Offers the HECM loan.

Depreciation

A decrease in a property's value. This term can also mean an appraisal made for the estimated loss of use of a property because of physical age, damage, or obsolescence, or it can refer to an annual tax deduction for wear and tear and loss of utility of property.

Durable power of attorney

A legal document that enables an individual to designate another person, called the attorney-in-fact, to act on his or her behalf, even in the event the individual becomes disabled or incapacitated.

Eminent domain

The right of a government to take private property for public use (and possibly private use for public benefit). A common example is taking private land for a public road. The owner must be fairly compensated.

Equity

The value of your home if you were to sell it, minus any debts you owe on it. For example, if you own a home worth $250,000 but still owe $75,000 on it, your home equity would be $175,000. Your reverse mortgage loan value is based partially on your equity.

Expected average mortgage interest rate

The mortgage interest rate used to calculate future payments to the borrower; it is established when the mortgage interest rate is established. For fixed-rate mortgages, it is the fixed mortgage interest rate. For adjustable rate mortgages, it is the sum of the lender's margin plus the weekly average yield for U.S. Treasury Securities adjusted to a constant maturity of ten years.

Fannie Mae
A government-sponsored company that operates privately to buy, sell, and make real estate–secured loans. Fannie Mae offers its own reverse mortgages, the Home Keeper Mortgage or Home Keeper for Home Purchase.

Federal Housing Administration (FHA)
An agency within the U.S. Department of Housing and Urban Development that administers many loan programs, loan guarantee programs, and loan insurance programs. FHA offers the Home Equity Conversion Mortgage (HECM).

Federally insured reverse mortgage
A reverse mortgage guaranteed by the federal government to ensure that the borrower always receives what the loan promises and to be sure the lender is repaid. The Home Equity Conversion Mortgage (HECM) is the only federally insured reverse mortgage.

Fee simple
The most common form of ownership in the United States, which provides the owner with absolute ownership to the entire property, including the right to dispose of the property during one's lifetime and to decide who receives the property after the owner's death.

FHA
See Federal Housing Administration.

Financial Freedom

One of the largest reverse mortgage lenders and servicers in the United States. Financial Freedom offers a proprietary Cash Account Advantage Plan reverse mortgage for seniors who have substantial home equity or higher-valued homes.

Financing

Rolling the costs of getting your loan (originator fees, closing costs, and so on) into the total loan balance in order to pay these extra costs along with your loan repayment. Many people opt to finance their fees, which can be several thousand dollars.

Fixed-rate mortgage

A loan secured by real property, featuring an interest rate that does not change during the term of the loan. A typical home mortgage is a 30-year fixed-rate mortgage. Long-term fixed-rate loans are not an option in reverse mortgages.

Hazard insurance

A form of insurance that protects against certain risks, such as fires and storms.

Home equity

See Equity.

Home Equity Conversion Mortgage (HECM)

By far the most popular reverse mortgage, the HECM is offered by the Federal Housing Administration (FHA), a division of HUD, and is insured by the federal government.

Home equity loan

A loan secured by a mortgage (typically a second mortgage) on one's principal residence, generally to be used for some non-housing expenditure. Typically reverse mortgages are secured by a first mortgage, but they may also be referred to as a home equity loan.

Home Keeper
Fannie Mae's reverse mortgage product, which offers higher loan limits than HECM and no mortgage insurance payment but often lower loan principal amounts when all factors are considered.

Home Keeper for Home Purchase
A spinoff of the Home Keeper, this loan is designed to use the reverse mortgage to help buy a new home.

Homeowners insurance
An insurance policy designed especially for homeowners. This insurance usually combines hazard coverage and liability coverage. Hazard coverage includes losses due to certain events, such as fire and storms. Liability coverage protects the property owner from claims arising from injuries or damage to other people or property.

House location survey
A scaled drawing of a property showing the property boundaries and the location of any structures on the property, such as house, shed, garage, and fence. Also referred to as an improvement location certificate.

HUD
The commonly used abbreviation for the United States Department of Housing and Urban Development, the department of the U.S. government established to implement certain federal housing and community development programs. This agency attempts to assure decent, safe, and sanitary housing for all Americans and investigates complaints of dis-

crimination in housing. FHA, which is a division of HUD, offers the HECM reverse mortgage loan product.

Improvement location certificate
A scaled drawing of a property showing the property boundaries and the location of any structures on the property, such as house, shed, garage, and fence. Also known as a house location survey.

Index
A published rate that represents the value of the securities that make it up, such as the 1-year Treasury Security Bill (T-Bill) rate. This number, plus a margin, equals your reverse mortgage interest rate.

Initial interest rate
The interest rate that is first charged on a HECM loan beginning at closing; it equals the 1-year U.S. Treasury Security rate, plus a margin.

Insured mortgage
A mortgage that has been insured. Such insurance is evidenced by the issuance of a mortgage insurance certificate.

Interest
The percentage of a sum of money charged by a lender on borrowed funds.

Leftover equity
In a reverse mortgage, leftover equity refers to the money left over from the sale of the home after your lender has been repaid.

Lender
A general term applied to any party that originates, holds, or funds loans.

Lien
A security interest granted against a property to secure the payment of a debt or the performance of some other obligation. Sometimes called an encumbrance. Generally all liens must be paid or removed from the property prior to obtaining a reverse mortgage. In many cases the proceeds from the reverse mortgage loan can be used to pay the lien.

Line of credit
Also called a credit line. This is an agreement wherein the lender promises to lend up to a certain amount without the need for the borrower to file for an additional application. A line of credit may require a minimum draw amount, and other rules may apply. A line of credit also typically allows the borrower to repay borrowed amounts at any time.

Living trust
A type of trust (also called an inter vivos trust) created to hold ownership of all or some of a person's assets during his or her life and to hold and/or distribute those assets after death.

Loan advances
All funds advanced or charged to a borrower's account pursuant to the loan agreement.

Loan balance
This dollar amount equals the amount owed on a loan, including interest and any fees that were financed with the loan.

Loan-to-value (LTV) ratio

The portion of the amount borrowed compared to the cost or value of the property; that is, mortgage debt divided by the value of the property. Lenders are often constrained as to the maximum loan-to-value ratio on loans they originate. For example, an 80 percent loan-to-value ratio on a $100,000 house would mean the borrower could receive an $80,000 loan on the property. Most reverse mortgages typically have an initial maximum loan-to-value ratio lower than that of a forward mortgage.

London Interbank Offered Rate (LIBOR) index

The rate at which banks lend money to each other in London, England, used by Financial Freedom to calculate your reverse mortgage interest rate.

Lump sum

One of three payment options for a reverse mortgage. If you choose a lump sum payment, you receive a check for the total loan amount at closing and manage it as you wish, but you will receive no additional money from your reverse mortgage.

Margin

The extra percentage points an originator or lender adds to the base interest rate (set by the government). Margins are capped differently for each loan but are generally between 1.5 and 5 percent.

Maturity

The due date of a loan; when the loan must be repaid.

Maximum claim amount

The lesser of the appraised value of the property and the maximum dollar amount for an area established by HUD.

This is normally the maximum amount that may be funded by HUD.

Medicaid

The federally funded U.S. health insurance program for individuals and families with low incomes and low resources. It is jointly funded by the states and federal government, and is managed by the states. Among the groups of people served by Medicaid are eligible low-income parents, children, seniors, and people with disabilities. Medicaid is the largest source of funding for medical and health-related services for people with limited income.

Medicare

The health insurance program funded by the federal government, generally for older Americans.

Mortgage

A loan that is secured by real estate. The term actually refers to a security interest creating a lien, whether called a mortgage, deed of trust, security deed, or another term used in the particular jurisdiction.

Mortgage insurance (MIP)

Associated with HECM loans, mortgage insurance protects you and the lender in case your loan balance grows higher than your home value (in which case the lender would lose money on your loan). The payment for this insurance is called a mortgage insurance premium (MIP) and is based on a percentage of your interest rate.

Negative amortization

An increase in the outstanding balance of a loan. In a reverse mortgage this results when additional amounts are advanced to the borrower and interest accrues. The result of negative amortization is a decrease in homeowner's equity.

Net principal limit
The amount of funds available over the course of the reverse mortgage.

Non-recourse loan
A loan secured by real property, but for which the borrower is not personally liable. In the event of a default, the lender is limited to the secured property to satisfy the debt but has no recourse against the other assets of the borrower. This describes all major reverse mortgages. It means that a reverse mortgage borrower can never owe more than the value of his or her home.

Note
The promissory note signed by the borrower acknowledging the borrower's promise to pay a debt.

One-month secondary market CD index
The interest rate Fannie Mae bases your rate on, as determined by the Board of Governors of the Federal Reserve System.

Origination (loan origination)
The process of making a new loan, from marketing the loan to closing.

Origination fees
Charges to a borrower to cover the cost of issuing the loan, such as credit checks, an appraisal, and title expenses.

Originator

The person who actually makes your loan a reality. Originators provide documents, help you choose the right loan, send all of your paperwork through to the lender, and answer any and all questions you may have along the way.

Planned unit development (PUD)

One of the housing types eligible for most reverse mortgages, a PUD consists of a subdivision or other project that shares common property (such as a community pool or clubhouse).

Plat

A plan or map of a specific land area. A subdivision plat is typically filed in the county clerk and recorder's office and shows a detailed image of the size and boundaries of each lot, easements, and location of utilities and streets; also lists covenants.

Prepayment penalty

A penalty for paying off a mortgage before it is due.

Principal

The loan amount before interest and other fees.

Principal balance

The sum of all loan advances, including unpaid interest and mortgage insurance premiums before interest, fees, or any other additions.

Principal limit

The maximum disbursement that could be received by the borrower in any month under a HECM reverse mortgage, taking into account the age of the youngest borrower, the interest rate, and the maximum claim amount. This amount may increase (and possibly decrease) during the term of the loan.

Principal residence

The dwelling where the borrower maintains his or her permanent place of abode, and typically spends the majority of the calendar year. A person may only have one principal residence at any one time. A property will normally be considered the principal residence of a borrower who is temporarily in a health-care institution, as long as the property is the principal residence of at least one other borrower who is not in a health-care institution.

Property tax deferral (PTD)

A type of state reverse mortgage, the PTD helps you pay your property taxes. This loan is a good choice if your sole reason for getting a reverse mortgage is to take care of these payments. PTDs are very inexpensive to get, and occasionally do not need to be repaid at all.

Proprietary reverse mortgage

Any reverse mortgage that is offered by a private company. The Fannie Mae Home Keeper, the Fannie Mae for Home Purchase, and the Financial Freedom Cash Account Advantage are all considered proprietary reverse mortgages.

Quit claim deed

This removes someone's name from the title or ownership of a property. For instance, if a child's name had been added on the title to their parent's home, the child needs to sign a quit claim deed to remove his or her name so the parents can obtain the reverse mortgage.

Repair addendum
If the appraiser recommends repairs, this document will be used to identify the specific repairs needed.

Required repairs
If noted in appraisal, these repairs must be completed; untreated damage could devalue property.

Reverse annuity mortgage
A reverse mortgage with a limited term, usually 10 years, which pays a fixed amount per month as income.

Reverse mortgage
A type of mortgage, designed primarily for homeowners 62 and over who have substantial equity in their home, by which a lender makes a lump sum payment or periodic payments to the borrower. The loan balance increases with interest and periodic payments over time, causing negative amortization. The non-recourse loan is repaid from proceeds from the future sale of the home.

Right of rescission
A borrower's right to cancel a reverse mortgage within three business days of closing if the reverse mortgage is covered by the Truth in Lending Act, Regulation Z, which gives consumers the right to cancel certain credit transactions that involve a lien on their principal dwelling.

Service set-aside
This sum is the value of the monthly servicing fee over the life of the loan.

Servicing

The maintenance on your loan after it closes (done by the servicer), which usually includes sending checks, updating information, changing your preferred payment options, providing you with regular statements to show how your reverse mortgage loan amount is growing, and processing day-to-day paperwork.

Servicing fee

Monthly fee charged by the lender for administering your account.

Shared equity mortgage

A home loan in which the lender is granted a share of the equity, thereby allowing the lender to participate in the proceeds from the sale of the property. Shared equity mortgages are not discussed in detail in this book.

Social Security

The U.S. social insurance program funded through dedicated payroll tax for the purpose of providing benefits during retirement, disability, and death.

Supplemental Security Income (SSI)

An income program for those over 65, which operates in addition to Social Security. SSI benefits may be affected by your reverse mortgage income.

Survey

The process by which a parcel of land is measured and its area determined; it can also mean a detailed map showing the measurements, boundaries, area, and contours of a parcel of land.

Tenure payments

Monthly equal payments throughout the life of the loan, which continue until you move out or die.

Tenure plan

Provides a predetermined amount of funds every month until the borrower no longer occupies the home as primary residence.

Term payments

Monthly equal payments that are paid for a specified amount of time.

Term plan

Provides equal monthly payments to borrower for a specific period of time.

Title

A legal document that proves ownership of a property. When you apply for a reverse mortgage, your originator orders a title search to make sure no one else holds any claims to your property.

Total annual loan cost (TALC) rate

The estimated cost of the reverse mortgage loan on an annual basis. This is a hypothetical projection, since you won't pay anything until the entire loan balance is due.

Truth in Lending Act (TILA)

A federal law designed to protect consumers in credit transactions by requiring clear disclosure of key terms of the lending arrangement and all costs. The regulations implementing the statute are known as Regulation Z.

United States Department of Housing and Urban Development
See HUD.

Variable rate
A rate that can change over the life of the loan. Variable rate is generally calculated as the following: Index + Margin = Interest Rate.

Viager
En viager means "for life." Viager is a private variation of reverse mortgage popular in France.

Index

About the Authors

Tammy Kraemer has been an attorney practicing business, real estate, and intellectual property law for almost ten years. She is currently in private practice. She worked in general counsel for a mid-size software company with worldwide offices. She also worked at a large regional law firm in their corporate law and securities department. She has written and edited numerous articles for newsletters and law journals. She lives in Colorado with her husband Tyler and their two children.

Tyler Kraemer has been an attorney in private practice focusing on estate planning, real estate, finance, and business law for almost ten years. His clients include lenders, borrowers, mortgage brokers, real estate brokers, real estate buyers and sellers, and business owners. Tyler has been a part of outside general counsel for the REALTOR® trade association and the for-profit multiple listing service, which included giving daily advice on homeowner issues. He has participated in National Association of REALTOR® conferences and workshops dealing with all facets of homeowner issues. He lives in Colorado with his wife Tammy and their two children.